REFINED BY

Fire

After you have
suffered
for a little while,
the God of
all grace,
who called you
to His
eternal glory
in Christ,
will Himself
perfect, confirm,
strengthen and
establish you.
1 PETER 5:10

"*Refined by Fire* is about courage, devotion, growth, and faith. It's about the character it takes to believe, the trust it takes to persevere, and the strength that results from this most fundamental of all human endeavors."
GENERAL ERIC K. SHINSEKI (USA RET.) AND MRS. PATTY SHINSEKI

★

"This is one of those 'I couldn't put it down' books. A *gripping* page-turner! Brian and Mel Birdwell are the *real* deal. Two people refined by an unimaginable crisis. As you read *Refined by Fire,* your own faith will be strengthened. You will laugh with them and cry with them. You will love this book and the Birdwells, just as I do!"
DENNIS RAINEY, PRESIDENT, FAMILYLIFE

★

"Gutsy, honest, and compelling. It shows what real faith—and true courage under fire—looks like in almost unimaginable circumstances. It also gives the rest of us a big-picture perspective on what really matters in everyday life."
ELLEN VAUGHN, FORMER V.P. OF EXECUTIVE COMMUNICATIONS FOR PRISON FELLOWSHIP AND AUTHOR OF *THE STRAND* AND *GIDEON'S TORCH,* COAUTHORED WITH CHARLES COLSON

★

"George Washington long ago said, 'The worth of one's character is measured by the trial of adversity.' On 9/11 most Americans witnessed the tragedy of the terrorist attacks from the outside, as observers. The Birdwells, however, witnessed it as participants. This inspiring, true story shows that the terrorist attack against the Pentagon did not *produce* character in the Birdwells; rather, it *revealed* their character."
DAVID BARTON, FOUNDER AND PRESIDENT OF WALLBUILDERS, A NATIONAL PRO-FAMILY ORGANIZATION

A Soldier's Story of 9-11

REFINED
by FIRE

A Family's Triumph of Love and Faith

LTC (RET) **BRIAN BIRDWELL**
& MEL BIRDWELL
with Ginger Kolbaba

Tyndale House Publishers, Inc.
WHEATON, ILLINOIS

Edited by Ramona Cramer Tucker

Published in association with the literary agency of The B & B Media Group, Inc., dba The Barnabas Agency, 109 S. Main, Corsicana, TX 75110; www.tbbmedia.com

Cover designed by Ron Kaufmann

Lyrics on p. 48 from the song "The Point of Grace" in *Songs of Ministry,* by worship leader Dennis Jernigan, are used by permission of Shepherd's Heart Music, Inc., P.O. Box 890358, Oklahoma City, OK 73189. 1-800-877-0406.

Library of Congress Cataloging-in-Publication Data

Birdwell, Brian.
    Refined by fire : a family's triumph of love and faith / Brian and Mel Birdwell, with Ginger Kolbaba.
        p. cm.
    ISBN 0-8423-8603-3
    1. Birdwell, Brian. 2. Birdwell, Mel. 3. Christian biography—United States.
4. September 11 Terrorist Attacks, 2001—Religious aspects—Christianity.
I. Birdwell, Mel. II. Kolbaba, Ginger. III. Title.
    BR1700.3.B57 2004
    277.3′083′0922—dc22   2004001579

Printed in the United States of America

11   10   09   08   07   06   05   04
 7   6   5   4   3   2   1

To the memory of
three great Americans—
Antoinette Sherman,
Cheryle D. Sincock,
*and **Sandra C. Taylor***—
who gave all at the Pentagon
on 9/11/2001

CONTENTS

FOREWORD

THE EVENTS OF SEPTEMBER 11, 2001, will forever be etched in our memories. For Brian and Mel Birdwell the etching goes deeper—to body and soul. In an instant, a nanosecond, their lives were turned upside down, never to be the same. The life-stealing thief came with a deafening explosion and a jet-fueled fireball. Brian was on fire, his body screaming out with the pain of being burned over 60 percent of his body.

This is their story—a gripping story of survival and victory, a story of God's faithfulness, a love story strengthened by the Refiner's fire.

Brian and Mel Birdwell are warriors. In 1984 Brian was commissioned as a lieutenant of Field Artillery, United States Army. In the Army he would learn about the warrior spirit and learn the truth about freedom—that freedom's never free. In 1987 this Texas boy married an Oklahoma girl, and they began their "Army life" together. You will hear firsthand about their painful upbringing and personal struggles. Little did they know that God would use these events to prepare them for the difficult days following September 11.

I met Brian and Mel when Brian "got pulled up" to be executive officer to Ms. Jan Menig, my outstanding deputy in the Army's Installation Management Office. From day one I could see that Brian and Mel were a team, a great Army family—raising their son, Matt, supporting other families, serving in their church, and growing in their relationship with Jesus Christ, their Lord and Savior. Many times Brian and I would talk about how God was working in our lives and share our love for Christ with each other. This, too, would be preparation for the days ahead.

I'll never forget my first visit to the Burn Unit. I saw Mel before going in to see Brian. We hugged and talked of God's sovereignty and comfort. Inside I was praying that God would strengthen her and Brian for the days ahead. Although I'd been to war in Desert Storm, I was not prepared for what I would see when I donned the sterile gear and went into Brian's room in the ICU. He was wrapped from head to ankle in gauze. I was so thankful he was alive but couldn't even imagine his pain and suffering. Little did any of us know what he would endure in over thirty operations and countless therapy sessions. There were—and still are—no words to express my feelings. Brian wanted to know about Sandi and Cheryle, our two wonderful "officemates" who were lost in the fire. These were tough days . . . and there would be many more.

Refined by Fire is far more than a tale of survival, although Brian would tell you he's a survivor, not a victim. It's about two modern-day heroes who understand that freedom's not free!

In the very worst of times Brian and Mel found that God was there for them—and that He was preparing them to comfort others. From this tragedy, Face the Fire Ministries, Inc. was born.

As you read Brian and Mel's remarkable journey, learning to walk with God day by day, your heart will be touched. You'll gain hope and perspective for your own life challenges. You'll find yourself saying, "Compared to what Brian and Mel went through, my problems and challenges are pretty insignificant." I certainly have.

May God draw you to Himself, speak to your heart, and bless you through this book.

★ *To Brian and Mel:*
I am honored to call you "friends." Thanks for telling your story. You have challenged me to "press on" and make every day count. God has a purpose!

In His grip,

R. L. Van Antwerp
Major General
United States Army

INTRODUCTION
A Day We'll Never Forget

"Terrorist attacks can shake the foundations of our biggest buildings,
but they cannot touch the foundation of America."
PRESIDENT GEORGE W. BUSH, September 11, 2001

★*Brian*

On September 11, 2001, American Flight 77 crashed into the Pentagon. I was standing fifteen to twenty yards from the point of impact. It took only a few seconds to change my life forever.

The searing second- and third-degree burns that were inflicted upon more than 60 percent of my body brought months of absolute torture. For weeks no one knew if I would live or die.

But God knew. He had a plan for my life. And no terrorist would be able to work against the purposes of God. My survival didn't happen by luck or mere chance. It happened because a sovereign God had a specific plan for my life. And while I do not understand why God chose to allow me to live when so many others perished, I do know that he was with me.

The course back toward living has been dark, difficult, and agonizing. There have been many moments when I cried out to God, "Why did you let me live?"

The answer always seemed to be *Just wait. Be patient.*

For three months I waited—and endured more than thirty excruciating surgeries, daily debridements, and torturous physical therapy. I waited through the long hours of lying alone with my thoughts and questions, revisiting the events of September 11 in all their horror again and again.

Through my experiences I learned a lot of lessons, the most important one being that God doesn't necessarily keep us from going through our own personal fire. He won't magically remove the hurt and the consequences of decisions made. But he promises to walk through those experiences with us. While he may not take away the pain, he gives us the strength, comfort, peace, and endurance to walk through, to get to the other side, and to be closer to God in the process.

Every tear we shed, God sheds so many more. When we're angry over injustices done to us, God is even angrier. When we grieve, he grieves. God is there with us each step of the way.

I am a survivor—but only by God's grace and compassion. I could never have gotten through this horrific ordeal without depending on Christ and without the support of my committed wife, Mel.

★ *Mel*

Before September 11, 2001, we were boring, normal, everyday people. We spent our Friday nights at home watching John Wayne movies and eating pizza. We attended church, got together with friends, and enjoyed our quiet, uneventful life as a family.

This is a true story about the Lord's sovereignty in our lives. Our lives are forever different. The day I went to the Pentagon and saw where Brian was in relation to where the plane struck, I realized that there was no way he could have survived—except for the hand of God protecting him and our family.

We've had many opportunities to speak about our faith. We think it's important to tell our story, because if we fail to do so, then those thousands of lives lost on that day were a waste, not a sacrifice.

Some parts of this book have been extremely difficult for us to write and to reread. We had blocked out so much of the pain that we didn't remember certain events until we began to reread my journal and then discuss and relive the ordeal.

No one can ever comprehend the horror and full impact of what Brian's body experienced, but we can share on the level of compassion and sympathy. This book isn't easy to read—it shows a portion of the pain, suffering, and indignities we endured.

And yet we also pray it shows the hope we have held onto and claimed as our own.

★*Brian and Mel*

We all face personal fires—those life-changing, traumatic times when the course of our lives are altered. Those are the times when we learn to rely on God—or when we decide to become angry with him and push him away. When we rely on him, he shows us what he's capable of accomplishing—regardless of the tragedy we may experience, whether it is physical, emotional, or spiritual.

While this book tells our story, it is so much more than that. It is really a story of God's love, mercy, graciousness, and loving sovereignty in our lives. He is at work in all of our life stories—sometimes he works in big, miraculous ways, and sometimes he works behind the scenes. But he is always working.

That is where our hope lies. Christ provides the hope that we will endure this suffering and emerge stronger because of it.

ONE

Death Blow

★ *Brian*

It was a day like any other at the Pentagon outside Washington DC.

I stepped out of the men's room on the second floor and started down Corridor 4 toward the outermost ring of the building, the E-Ring. The hall of the newly renovated wedge was lit with bright fluorescents in the ceiling panels. Everything was a stark white, sterile, and quiet. No one else was around as I headed back to my office.

It was 9:37 A.M., Tuesday, September 11, 2001.

I took seven or eight steps and was in front of the first set of elevators when *bang!* There was a deafening explosion.

Where had the sound come from?

It wasn't the jackhammers of the remodeling crew, even though I'd heard them frequently in that wedge of the Pentagon. And after spending nineteen years in the Army—being a Gulf War veteran and having more than ten years as an artillery officer—I was familiar with loud explosions, concussions, and other noises of war. This was louder than anything I'd heard in my lifetime. This was the crashing resonance of metal slamming through concrete—a scraping, screaming, high-pitched, thunderous blast.

Everything happened at once, in less than an instant—a nanosecond. Yet everything seemed in slow motion. *Bomb!* I thought as I started to take another step.

Immediately everything around me went pitch black, as if I was thrown into a deep, dark cave. A loud *whoosh* blasted toward me. Fire exploded at and around me, slamming me across the hall, ripping my glasses from my face, and then tossing me limply onto the floor. I heard debris flying around me. The ceiling panels and light fixtures crashed down; the walls shook as if hit by an earthquake. But I couldn't see anything, except for a ring of yellow surrounding me. Then I realized . . . I was on fire!

The pain came instantly. The heat was so intense that the polyester pants of my uniform melted into my legs. My arms, back, legs, face, and hair were alight with flames.

Thick smoke engulfed me, slapping me across the face and threatening to suffocate me. I swallowed it as I gasped for air. My mind registered a distinct odor and taste. *Jet fuel?* I gulped and choked on the heavy vapors and the dust from the building debris as I struggled just to get oxygen.

It was hard to keep my eyes open—the smoke and heat from the fire stung my eyes. I didn't know where the fire was coming from, where the explosion had happened. All I could see was the intense glow of yellow right in front of my face and then around it, total blackness.

My body screamed in pain, but there was nothing to put out the flames.

I'm not sure how long I lay on the floor. It seemed like an eternity, but it was probably only five or ten seconds.

I forced my eyes to open. I tried to get to my feet, but my body wouldn't cooperate. In order to survive whatever this was, I knew I needed to escape—fast.

But which way do I go? Which way to safety? I wondered. I was so disoriented from the blast that I didn't even know which way I was facing after I had been thrown. Was I facing safety or more danger?

It doesn't matter, I told myself. *You just need to get away.*

I tried hard not to panic, yet it was difficult to stay focused when the pain was so intense and all I could see was that yellow ring of fire with the black around it.

Then there was the awful noise around me—as overwhelming and full of static as though someone was strumming an electric guitar at the highest decibel. Fire alarms added to the shrill sound. I was trying not to pay attention to anything except getting away from the fire, but the cumulative noise pierced my concentration. Worse, I couldn't bring my hands up to cover my ears because I was trying to use them to get off the floor.

I tried to stand four or five times, using my hands and my arms to get up. I'd manage to get on one knee, then I'd fall. My legs wouldn't support me, and I had no balance. The concussion had damaged my inner ear equilibrium. And because it was so black around me, I lost all sense of depth.

I tried desperately to see something—*anything*—other than the oval of yellow surrounding me. But there was nothing. No wall, no doors, no elevator, nothing. It was as though there was nothing to touch except for whatever I was lying on.

Finally the pain was too much to bear. I tried to stand one last time and fell sideways. In my anguish I screamed, "Jesus! I'm coming to see you!"

I knew I was going to die. As a soldier I'd been trained never to give up. But I did. I didn't try to get up again. Instead, I thought, *Okay, Lord, if this is the end for me, if this is the way I am to die, then okay.*

I shut my eyes and thought about what a horrific death this was. Then I thought about Mel, my wife, and our son, Matt. My mind recalled the events of the morning before I left for work. Did they know what was happening to me? I didn't want this morning to be the last time I'd ever see them. I remembered saying good-bye to them just a few hours earlier, never dreaming that I might not come home again. What would their lives be like without me around?

This is it, I realized. *I won't see them again. . . .*

★ *Mel*

For Matt, our twelve-year-old son, and me, September 11 began as a normal day, complete with homeschooling. Earlier that year, because of some classroom situations in Matt's public school, we had decided to take him out for a year to homeschool him.

While we were working on a science experiment, my friend Joyce phoned. "Mel, a plane just smashed into the World Trade Center!" Matt and I moved into the living room and flipped on the television for a bit. We watched as the second plane flew into the other tower. Matt kept asking me questions, but I could only answer, "Honey, I have no idea what is going on."

It never dawned on me that what we'd just seen on television might be a terrorist attack.

I wanted to keep watching, but I was also homeschooling. "Okay,

Matt, let's get back to your studies," I told him and turned off the television. We'd just finished an experiment using pie pans and water to show how water evaporates and leaves a residue behind. We were so excited that this experiment had actually worked since Matt and I weren't too great at science experiments. We'd even left the pie pan sitting out to re-enact our successful experiment for Brian later that evening when he arrived home.

Matt and I moved back to the kitchen island to work on our history lesson.

Actually, as I thought about it later, I realized how odd it was that we turned off the television. Normally I wouldn't have done that. I would have phoned or e-mailed Brian at work to give him the news. Yet for some reason I had an uneasy feeling about calling him.

We were in the middle of history when our neighbor Sara called. "Is your TV on?" she asked. Her voice sounded panicky.

"No, we're working on history."

"The Pentagon has been hit."

I nearly dropped the phone. I couldn't believe it. I yelled to Matt, "The Pentagon has been hit!" and raced toward the television.

It felt as if I were running in slow motion to get to that television.

I flipped it on and watched in horror as giant flames shot from the gaping hole in the side of the Pentagon. The news showed an aerial view of the flames everywhere and the black smoke spewing from the building.

Then I spotted the Pentagon air traffic control tower and helipad. Behind it I could see the blazing fire and smoke.

I gasped. *Oh no. No, no, no!*

Matt kept saying, "Mom, that's not Dad's side of the building! Dad is on the other side of the building! It's *not him."*

But I knew the truth. Brian's office was behind that helipad—and his window had flames coming out of it. Brian's department had just moved into that newly renovated wedge of the Pentagon eight to ten weeks earlier. When he'd moved in, I had gone with him to help unpack boxes. I had sat at his desk and watched the rain fall on that helipad. I had looked out that window that now had flames spitting from it.

"Mom," Matt said, increasingly looking scared, "that's *not* Dad!"

"Honey, I pray you're right," was all I could say. I felt in my heart he wasn't right. But what could I say to him? "No, Matt, you're wrong"? I knew that no matter what happened, I had to be strong for my son. I couldn't fall apart.

Yet all I really wanted to do was to start screaming. For us, for Brian. Instead, with a calm that was not my own, I said, "Matt, honey, let's pray for Dad."

I've never prayed so hard in my life. We prayed for Brian to be safe, for him not to be in the office, for him to be out running an errand, retrieving documents, in a meeting, even getting a doughnut for his boss! Something, *anything*. Just please, *please* don't let him be in his office.

After Matt and I prayed, I tried to call Brian's office, and the phone rang and rang, as if nothing had happened and yet all of the people were suddenly gone. It was creepy. Then I called Brian's cell phone. While I knew he wouldn't have his cell phone on because it didn't work inside the thick walls of the Pentagon, I was hoping against hope that, for some reason, he might have turned it on. When I got his voice mail, I hung up.

We were glued to the television set. The more I watched the gruesomeness, the enormity of what had happened, the more my heart told me this wasn't going to be a good outcome. I sat on the couch and knew that if Brian had been sitting at his desk or in his department, he was now standing at the throne of God. We would never see him again.

My mind battled between staying calm and going hysterical. I knew I couldn't think the worst or I would fall apart. So I called my friend Debbie Vance, who attends our church, and explained that I was sure we were in big trouble. Then I asked her to come over. I needed a friend for comfort and support, someone just to sit with me. I also asked her to call our church and tell our pastors that Brian was in the area of the Pentagon that had been hit and to ask them to pray for him.

While we waited for Debbie to arrive, Matt started to melt down. He became overwhelmed with the realization of what was happening and began punching the walls in the dining room. He cried. He yelled. He groaned. He paced back and forth around the house. And he kept telling me, "No, Dad's okay. It's not his side of the building. He's fine. *Fine.*"

It was gut-wrenching to watch him. No twelve-year-old should have to go through what our son did. No mom should have to watch, helpless. It was agonizing to feel so intensely powerless.

While we waited for any word, I phoned Brian's mom, his brother, Wade, and my best friend, Karen, in North Carolina. I told them that Brian's area had been hit, but that was all I knew.

That was the most difficult—not knowing. I was watching my husband's office burning and had no idea where he was or how he was. I needed to know what had happened to him. I needed to know he was alive.

Just then the doorbell rang. It was one of my neighbors, who wanted to offer support but didn't know what to say. We stood awkwardly silent at the door for a few minutes, then I told him I needed to get back to the television, to see if the newscasters had any more details.

Finally Matt couldn't take it anymore. "I have to get out of here," he said and ran out of the house.

I called my sister, Connie. I was pretty calm talking to everybody else—I was able to give them what details I knew to get through the conversations. But as soon as Connie answered the phone, I started to sob.

"I don't know how I can do this without Brian," I cried. "I don't think he's going to survive this. What am I going to do? How are Matt and I going to go on? How is Matt going to go on without a dad?" We both sobbed uncontrollably on the phone. But when Matt returned, I wiped my eyes, told Connie I needed to go, then tried to pull myself together.

We waited and watched TV for another two hours. While we waited to hear news of Brian, Matt took several walks. And all the while I kept praying—praying for the best but thinking the worst.

★ *Brian*

I'd stopped moving. *This is the end*, I thought. I was still gasping for air; it felt as if I'd opened an oven door and was breathing in the hot air. Yet I wouldn't struggle anymore—even though the fire and pain seared through my body. At that moment the building became absolutely quiet to me. I didn't hear the shrill, blaring sounds still screeching around me.

I lay on the floor and wondered when my soul would depart from my body—and what it would feel like. While I didn't know exactly what to expect, I knew it had to be better than what I was currently enduring. As I focused on eternity, I was enveloped by an absolute silence, an absolute peace . . . as if what was happening in the building wasn't really happening. I was separated from everything going on around me. God was in that place with me—it was just him and me. And while the pain was excruciating, I felt indescribable peace.

I waited to see the light of that tunnel into eternity, which I'd heard so many people with near-death experiences discuss. So I waited.

And waited.

But the light never came.

I lay there waiting, with my face toward the ground. While it may have taken no more than two minutes, it felt like hours. I had no sense of time or space. I started to think, *Okay, Lord. Come on. Let's get on with this thing. What are you waiting for? I'm here. I'm ready.*

Suddenly, on the left side of my face, I felt something trickle past my eye and run down my cheek. It wasn't a huge gush, just a small stream. It wasn't warm, so I knew it wasn't blood. It was cold; it was water. Somehow I had landed under one of the working sprinkler systems, and the sprinkler began dousing the fire that was consuming me.

My face was the only place I could feel the water. Because of my sensory overload, the rest of my body was reacting as if I were completely numb, so I didn't know if I was wet anywhere else. I just knew I was no longer on fire.

Smoke still swirled around me; nothing had changed. But with the touch of that water, everything changed: My courage was renewed to try to escape again.

I opened my eyes. My face was pointed toward the ground. As I looked around at floor level I could see large pieces of sheet rock, splintered two-by-fours, glass, aluminum framing, ceiling panels, lighting fixtures, electrical wiring everywhere.

I could see the floor because the smoke was still above me, so I glanced behind me. It was black. Then I looked in front of me and saw a dim light in the distance, down a long stretch of corridor. It was like being out at sea and seeing a fog lamp but not the source of the lamp; you just see the effects of it. While I couldn't see where the light was coming from, I could see its effects on the floor.

I knew I was in the corridor, in close proximity to the point of impact. I sensed that I was still close to the bathroom.

Somehow I was able to get some of my bearings. I squinted down the corridor behind me toward the E-Ring and could see the total darkness.

Suddenly I was reoriented. The fire was out around me. *Okay, I'm not dead yet,* I thought, *so now I need to get to medical attention—quickly.*

The rest of the corridor filled with black smoke. I knew now I had to move rapidly toward the light, which I figured was toward the A-Ring, toward the inner court of the Pentagon. Since I was between the D- and E-Rings, the A-Ring was at least fifty yards away, half the length of a football field. And everything was completely dark.

I took a deep breath, coughed, and tried to get to my feet again. This time it didn't seem to take as much effort. I reached out my arm and located a wall beside me, which I used to hoist myself up. I determined I was lying next to the far wall, across from the bathroom.

I still had trouble balancing, and I bounced into the walls. But slowly I began to stagger, stiffly groping my way down the corridor, over the rubble, and toward the light.

There was enough light for me to see the damage to my arms. I saw a large chunk of skin dangling from my left arm. Mostly my arm was black. Not only was I burned, I was covered with ash, dirt, soot, and debris.

My survival instincts clicked on again. I tried not to think about what I'd seen hanging from my arm.

In the meantime I struggled to breathe. My lungs had been burned from the intense heat, and I had inhaled aerosolized fuel. I could taste the jet fuel in my mouth. I breathed in smoke, choking and coughing. Even though I was breathing, my body was still being deprived of oxygen, as if I was holding my breath. It felt like someone had knocked the wind out of me. I tried to suck in the oxygen, but I just couldn't get any.

My adrenaline kicked in. I realized that while I was no longer on fire, I was still in serious trouble. I started to stagger more quickly—almost frantically—over or around the debris. Once I started moving down the corridor away from the smoke, there was still enough light for me to see more of the extent of the damage from the concussion and blast. Flimsy ceiling tiles flapped around, and other light fixtures and electrical lines dangled dangerously.

I knew I had to walk straight down the closed corridor; I couldn't enter any of the other rings to reach safety because each ring could be accessed only with a special security badge. I wasn't cleared for those rings, and anyway, my badge was cooked.

As I worked my way toward the B-Ring, I noticed I couldn't see the escalators at the end of the corridor in the A-Ring.

This is bad, I realized. The fire door between the B-Ring and A-Ring had been closed. Behind me was the point of impact. To my front, the fire door. To my left all access doors were locked. To my right everything was still covered by the renovation plywood from the areas under construction.

There was no escape.

TWO

Road to Survival

★*Brian*

I made it all the way to safety, and there is no safety! I thought. *This can't be happening!*

I knew my second chance at life was over. I was trapped and now was forced to wait helplessly for the rapidly approaching fire and smoke to catch up to me.

In the newly renovated section of the Pentagon, they had installed automated fire doors to ensure that if a fire broke out in that corridor, it would be unable to spread to the rest of the building. It was certainly doing its job for the building; the fire wouldn't be able to spread through the Pentagon. But it wasn't good for me. I couldn't get out.

I didn't know what I was going to do—and the smoke from the point of impact was rushing down the corridor, making it impossible to find any good air.

Then suddenly, unexpectedly, a locked door to the B-Ring opened.

Out came Colonel Roy Wallace, who stepped into the corridor to see if he could work his way around the building.

Once he opened the access door, he noticed the dense smoke. And he noticed me. From his startled look, I must have seemed ghastly. I was black from the burns and the soot. Sections of my pants were either gone or had melted into my skin. The back of my shirt was completely gone; the front was still there and soaked in blood. And I was soaking wet from the sprinklers, which before now I hadn't realized.

Next, Lieutenant Colonel Bill McKinnon stepped into the corridor. I recognized him immediately. Bill and I knew each other as students at Command and General Staff College in Fort Leavenworth, Kansas. We started our assignments at the Pentagon on the same day. Many days we would go to the Pentagon Officers' Athletic Club (POAC) to work out, or we'd run together and talk about the events of the day.

Roy started toward me as I saw Bill. *I'm saved!* I thought with relief as I collapsed at Roy's feet. Bill yelled behind him, "Hey, guys, come here! We've got one out here." That was a shock—while I recognized Bill, he didn't recognize me. *What do I look like?* I wondered.

Six officers rushed toward me and began to pick me up. As they lifted me, the pain became unbearable. "Put me down! Put me down!" I yelled. "No, don't touch me! It hurts!" I grabbed Bill's shirt with my right hand and saw that my hand was bloody; shreds of skin were falling off my fingers. My arms were burned all the way up to my armpits. I felt cooked, like a hot dog that's been on the grill too long. The inside may still be meaty, but the outside is blackened and hard. So when you touch the outside, it begins to flake off.

As I kept screaming for them not to touch me, they grasped hands with each other underneath my back and legs. They moved me into the B-Ring office area and began to walk quickly to safety and medical help.

I began to shout at Bill, "Call Mel! Call Mel and tell her I'm alive." But Bill didn't know who I was. He couldn't recognize me, and he couldn't read any of my IDs. Both my identification/access badge and my metal nametag that was pinned to my uniform shirt were melted and covered with blood. But the whole time they were moving me I kept shouting to Bill, "Call Mel!" and then, "Put me down!"

It seemed as if the pain was worse than when I was on fire. Maybe it was because I knew at this point I wasn't dying, so I was able to concentrate on the pain. Earlier, the pain was irrelevant because I knew my death was imminent. But this time I hurt because the men were now using burned parts of my body to hold my entire body weight.

The officers moved me from the B-Ring of Corridor 4 to the A-Ring between Corridors 5 and 6, which was about fifty to sixty yards. The A-Ring is the innermost ring of the Pentagon; it opens into the courtyard. The officers took me to the Redskins snack bar, which had become an informal gathering place where some personnel from the Pentagon clinic had set up a medical triage area. I knew we couldn't stay there long because it was damaged by the fire and flooding from the sprinkler system. The sprinklers were still going off, and the fire alarms were still blaring. The electricity had been cut from most of that section of the building, so we were moving in partial darkness, except for the light coming through the Kevlar-coated, green-yellow-tinted windows. It wasn't as black as in the corridor, but it was still eerily dark. Most of the people had evacuated the building to the inner courtyard or out of the Pentagon completely.

When they finally set me down by a staircase that leads into the center main courtyard in the A-Ring, it seemed as if medical staff were there immediately. To keep my mind off the pain, I tried to focus on my surroundings. Since we were right by a staircase that led from the third, fourth, and fifth floors down to the first floor, hundreds of people were scrambling down the staircase to get out of the building and into the courtyard.

I noticed there were already three other injured people at the triage area, and then another one or two joined us. I couldn't see the other people's injuries, but I was able to get a better sense of what kind of shape I was in.

My face was already puffing; I could feel the swelling. And my eyes were beginning to swell shut. But I could see enough to recognize I was severely burned.

I'd been burned badly on my leg while I was stationed in Korea in 1985 when a hot-water hose burst off a spigot and gave me second-degree burns. I remember seeing the blistered skin where I'd been burned.

This was different; this was worse than that. There was no redness to my skin or even a tint of light to dark red. Most of my skin was just gone. And what little skin was left was charred black.

I looked down at my injuries, then began to tremble severely. I was in shock.

★*Mel*

What is taking so long? I wondered. *Why haven't I heard anything yet?*

I kept watching the television and waiting—and still nothing. Not one word. The wait was unbearable.

Matt went for another walk. While he was gone I prayed for Brian's safety and the others in his office. *Lord, please keep the others safe. Let them be okay. Let Brian be okay.*

I wondered where my friend Debbie was and when she would arrive. I needed someone there with me.

Then all of a sudden, the damaged area of the Pentagon collapsed. As I watched the television, I fell to my knees in horror and cried out, "Oh, God, NO!!! No, no!" My chest felt so heavy I could hardly breathe. "Please, God, please!" I wept and pled. "I can't make it without Brian. Please!"

★ *Brian*

"Call Mel! Call my wife! Tell her I'm okay," I kept yelling in the make-shift triage area.

A lady who was working in that area asked me, "What's your name?"

"Brian Birdwell," I replied.

That's when Bill McKinnon found out who I was. His face went white, and immediately he said, "Brian! Man, what's your phone number? I'll get ahold of Mel." I gave him the number, which he tried to dial. But all the phone circuits were jammed.

Then Dr. John Baxter, an Air Force colonel and flight detachment physician, who was the senior medical person, along with several other military personnel—Specialist Kris Sorenson, Corporal Dan Nimrod, and Colonel Robin Davitt—began to evaluate my condition and tend to my wounds.

Blood was all over me. My light green uniform shirt was covered, as if I had dunked it in a pool of blood.

With all the soot and blood, Dr. Baxter didn't know if I had puncture wounds from flying debris such as the steel or glass or if it was just the blood from being a skinned person.

Dr. Baxter asked, "Brian, are you hurt other than the burns? What do you think your other injuries are? Do you have any broken bones?"

I told him, "I don't think I'm hurt other than the burns. I don't feel as if there's anything broken."

Then he began to poke at different places on my body. "Can you feel this?" he would ask.

Dr. Baxter noticed that my shoes were still on my feet. I was wearing leather Florsheim shoes, which, miraculously, held up in the fire. So he took off my shoes, then cut what was left of my pants completely up the legs. He determined my feet were about the only places on my body that were unscathed. Even my ankles didn't survive without burns—I had burn rings where my socks burned as they disintegrated. They weren't even there! So my legs and ankles were charred black, while my feet were rosy pink and healthy.

Dr. Baxter grabbed some morphine and an IV unit from his medical bag. He gave me a shot of the morphine through my right foot to help alleviate some of the pain.

At the same time, they needed to put an IV in my left foot. That was Colonel Davitt's job. She hadn't put in an IV in years and was concerned about inserting it correctly and not hurting me more. But there was no one else who was available to do it. "I have to hit this vein just right," she said nervously. "This is harder since it's in your foot."

Fortunately she hit the vein perfectly the first time. Not that I would have noticed anyway because of the intense pain in the other areas of my body.

While Colonel Davitt inserted the IV, a woman ran down the stairs to escape. But when she saw me lying there, she felt led to pray with me. So she came to my side and knelt beside my head. By the look on her face when she saw my injuries, I was struck again by how serious my condition must be. She asked my name, then told me, "Brian, my name is Natalie. I feel impressed to pray with you. Would that be all right?"

"Yes, please!" I couldn't believe a Christian was there beside me. Natalie helped calm me while the triage personnel were working to get me ready to evacuate. Even more, she had thought to grab her Bible before she left her desk. Now she opened her Bible, and we began to recite the Twenty-third Psalm, then the Lord's Prayer together. I spoke those words with such fervor. I knew that although I had survived the blast, I was still very much in danger of death. And the manner of my death was filling my thoughts.

I lay there trembling. My body was in shock. But my mind was still good and very active. I didn't feel that much pain anymore, probably because I was so concerned about how I was going to die: I wanted to die a dignified death in which I didn't panic but trusted God to maintain my composure.

"Please call my wife," I said again.

"Of course I will, Brian," Natalie said as she wrote down my phone number in her Bible.

Then she began to read Psalm 91 to me:

He who dwells in the shelter of the Most High
will abide in the shadow of the Almighty.
I will say to the Lord, "My refuge and my fortress,
my God, in whom I trust!"
For it is He who delivers you from the snare of the trapper
and from the deadly pestilence.
He will cover you with His pinions,
and under His wings you may seek refuge;
his faithfulness is a shield and bulwark.

You will not be afraid of the terror by night,
or of the arrow that flies by day;
of the pestilence that stalks in darkness,
or of the destruction that lays waste at noon.
A thousand may fall at your side
and ten thousand at your right hand,
but it shall not approach you.
You will only look on with your eyes
and see the recompense of the wicked.

Someone suggested to Nimrod and Sorenson, "Go get some ice out of the Redskin snack bar."

Nimrod and Sorenson went to get ice but didn't bring it back because ice isn't the best thing to do for burn survivors. You don't put ice on burns because the ice sticks to the tissue, and then it just peels off more tissue layers. All it will do is insulate the heat inside you and continue to cook you.

If I had only a small burn, they could have gotten cold water to help the burn cool. But because my burn was so major, they wanted to make sure those burned parts of my body were stuck out in the open to allow the heat to dissipate and leave my body.

So they put just enough wrapping on me to protect my burn areas, basically just to lightly cover my burns.

Natalie continued to pray over me. While the others were working on me with the IV and evaluating the level of my injuries, I paid attention to Natalie. I didn't concentrate on what Dr. Baxter or the others were doing to me.

Sorenson knelt beside me at my face level on one side. Natalie was right next to him. I recognized Sorenson immediately because just a week before I had gone for my annual "after forty years old" Army physical. I'd gone for the lab work, and Sorenson was the guy who drew the blood. Unfortunately the lab sample didn't make it to the computer, so I had to give blood a second time—and Sorenson drew the sample again.

As soon as I saw him beside me, I said, "Some way to give blood this time, isn't it, Sorenson?" He looked at me confused because he didn't recognize me. He simply covered me loosely with a blanket.

Nimrod was on my left, and Colonel Davitt and Colonel Baxter were at my feet.

While they were all working, I concentrated on listening to Natalie as she read comforting Scriptures and then prayed for me.

I again blurted out my phone number and asked her to contact Mel. She promised she would make sure Mel knew I was okay.

Within minutes of arriving at that area, I was prepped for the hospital. Once the "ambulance" arrived, they brought over a gurney. Natalie had just finished praying with me, then Dr. Baxter let her know they were getting ready to move me.

They turned me on my side, stuck a body board underneath me, picked me up, placed me on the gurney, and then into a golf-cart-sized Pentagon ambulance to rush me toward the area where the hospital ambulance was supposed to be waiting.

"Please don't forget to call my wife!" I shouted to Natalie.

"I won't forget," she said back.

Again I was struck by how serious my condition must be. I was the first person evacuated. I knew from experience that meant I was also the one in the worst shape.

★ ★ ★

Because I was still conscious through the entire ordeal, I felt it was important to know where I was and try to concentrate on what was happening. I'm not sure why. Maybe it was because I needed to have some sense of control. While my eyes were swollen and kept watering, I was still able to see things out of the sides of my eyes.

I knew I'd been put on the golf cart and that we had started in the A-Ring by Corridors 5 and 6. I watched as we passed the Korean War Memorial and wound our way down corridors, through parking garage-type loops, and finally came out at the Corridor 8 exit, which was almost directly on the other side of the building. We drove outside to the north parking lot. And at that point my eyes had swollen almost to the point of being completely closed.

The driver stopped outside at the northeast side of the building and dropped me off to wait for an official ambulance or medevac helicopter.

And there I lay, helpless, with the sun from the bright, cloudless morning sky beating down on my already cooked face. I was grateful when a woman came and held an umbrella over me to shield me from the sun.

★ ★ ★

As I lay on that gurney, unable to move, in incredible pain, time seemed to stop. I wondered, *What's taking so long?* Everything up to that point had gone so quickly. Medical officers had rushed to take care of me, and then I'd been driven quickly out to the north parking lot. So why was I waiting here? *Shouldn't someone be rushing me to the hospital by now?* I thought.

I couldn't see much of the scene taking place outside, but I could hear it. There was still chaos. Thousands of people streamed out into the north parking area. Sirens blared; people screamed and cried.

Then some police officers or some authority figures began announcing, "There's another plane coming! Get away from the building!"

I heard the word *plane*, and everything sunk in. The explosion and my lying out on the gurney near death were connected to the World

Trade Center plane crashes that I'd watched on television with my co-workers before I left for the men's room. The terrorists had crashed a plane into the Pentagon as well.

When people heard the warning, some started to scream, and the person holding the umbrella over me threw the umbrella aside and took off running. I wanted to run too—but I couldn't even move.

Just then Natalie emerged from that side of the building and saw what had happened. She hadn't followed me; she had gone out the pedestrian pathway. But we ended up in the same general vicinity. Somehow she spotted my stretcher and immediately came to me. She had tried to call Mel but couldn't get through since all the cell and land phone lines were overloaded. She began to pray with me some more, encouraging me.

I heard a lot of sirens going by, but I didn't know if they were ambulances or police cars. And no vehicle stopped to pick me up. Finally Natalie and a few other people decided to move me closer to the road for better access to an ambulance. Someone called out to about six military personnel nearby to help push the stretcher.

By the grace of God, I knew one of the officers, Major John Collison, whose office was in another part of the Pentagon. But just like Bill McKinnon, John didn't recognize me.

I was getting rolled around a lot, down the road toward Arlington Cemetery and on the grassy area near the parking lot. It seemed as though we kept going and going but not getting anywhere.

Finally we stopped, quite a distance from the building. An Air Force tech, Sergeant Reservist Jill Hyson, showed up to help. Jill worked as an X-ray technician but was doing her regulation two weeks of training at the Pentagon.

She took the toe tag that was on one of my feet. The toe tag listed my name and the medical procedures Dr. Baxter had performed on me. That tag was used to ensure that the emergency room physician would know what I had been given.

Jill began to take my vital signs and write them down. Then she handed the tag to Lieutenant Colonel Mike Bouchard and said, "Hang on to this. These are the vital signs, name of the casualty, and other information. We need to give this to the staff at the emergency room when we get there."

We started across the grass again and apparently Bouchard, who worked in the same department as Collison, looked at the paper and read my name. He tapped Major Collison on the shoulder and whispered, "Look at this paper. Look who this is."

He handed the tag to Collison, who stared at my face but still must not have believed it. Collison whispered back, "No way."

"It is," Bouchard insisted. "Look at the paper."

After a moment Collison grabbed my bandaged left hand and said in a shaky voice, "Sir, this is Major Collison. I'm here."

Those simple words were the most comforting thing for me. I was still afraid. I knew I wasn't in good shape. But John's presence calmed me.

"All right," I said. "That's great."

Then I squinted at him; his face had turned white with shock. "John," I said, "go with me to the hospital. I want you to go with me."

"Roger, Sir," John answered. "I'll stay with you the whole time."

He continued to hold my bandaged hand while they moved me to the road where an ambulance could pick me up. Still no vehicle came.

Most of the ambulances had driven around to the south side of the building, the closest point to where the explosion had taken place and also where the helipad was located. We were in north parking, on the opposite side of the building.

We waited about fifteen minutes until Shirley Baldwin, a nurse from the Pentagon's medical clinic, found me. She briefly assessed my injuries and looked at my IV running from my foot. "This is too low," she said to a medic nearby. "This man needs to be hydrated immediately. Give me another IV!"

"We don't have one," the medic said.

"Well, go into the building and get another one. Now!"

Her urgent tone made me afraid. "Ma'am," I asked her, "am I going to die?"

I noticed a moment's hesitation before she leaned over and told me, "You're going to be okay. We're going to get you to the hospital. Just hang on." I believed her because the look on her face said she believed it. I didn't know until later that she'd never told a patient that before.

A few moments later somehow the IV fell out of my foot. I couldn't see what was going on, but I could tell by the tone of a nurse's announcement that losing that IV was bad for me. Very bad.

Shirley told the people around my gurney, "Look, I know they called for an ambulance for this man more than a half hour ago. But we're not getting anything over here because they're all on the other side of the building."

Someone suggested flagging down a vehicle to take me to the hospital. And that's exactly what Shirley did. She commandeered a Jeep. Immediately Collison, Bouchard, and Colonel Robert Cortez opened the back door, collapsed my stretcher, and tried to push me into the back. But the back wasn't deep enough to accommodate my body board. They took me off the stretcher—keeping me on the body board—and tried to load me in, but my feet were sticking out.

"This isn't going to work," someone shouted. "Take him out! Let's flag down another vehicle."

So out I went and waited for another vehicle.

Immediately Shirley spotted Army Captain Wineland, who was trying to drive his White Ford Expedition out of the parking lot.

"Get that one!" She said. "That will work."

One of the officers flagged him down, walked up to the SUV, and told Wineland, "Your service is demanded. Take your vehicle, pull it over here next to this officer, and dump your stuff from the back of your vehicle out on the grass. You're going to drive him to the hospital."

Captain Wineland pulled up his vehicle next to me, and before he could get out of the Expedition, three guys had opened the back, jumped in, and started pitching everything—including golf clubs and other expensive items—out onto the grass next to the main road.

The captain jumped out and helped Collison, Brouchard, and Cortez maneuver me into the back. Then Jill jumped into the Expedition and sat on my left. John jumped into the vehicle and sat on my right. Again, with John sitting next to me, I felt the comfort of knowing someone was there with me who knew me. I wanted to know that if I was going to die, somebody I knew, who knew me, would be there and be able to tell Mel what happened.

Breathing was becoming extremely difficult. I could feel mucus or debris from the explosion coming out of my nose and throat. Since I was shaking so badly, they decided to put a space blanket over me to keep me warm. However, we quickly realized that was a bad decision because the blanket was sticking to my skin and cooking me still further. They immediately threw off the blanket—taking a chunk of my skin with it. The intense jet fuel odor filled that Expedition—not that I could smell it—or anything else—since my nostrils were fried. But I knew it had to be strong since several people kept commenting about it.

When everyone was situated in the Expedition, Lieutenant Colonel Bouchard handed Major Collison the paper with all my information on it. Then I heard all the doors shut. We were ready to go, but we didn't move.

Captain Wineland said, "Where are we going?"

Just then a Navy enlisted man pulled up on a motorcycle.

"What's going on?" he asked. "Do you need some help?"

I could barely see Jill out of the corner of my eye. She yelled, "We have a casualty, and he's critical. We're going to Georgetown!"

"I know where that is," the motorcyclist said.

"Then let's go!" Jill yelled. "Lead the way!"

★*Mel*

About two hours later the phone rang.

"Hello?" I said, hoping for news of Brian.

"Is this Mel Birdwell?" the man's voice asked on the other end.

"Yes, it is. Who is this?"

It seemed as if the man was taking forever to talk to me. I wanted to blurt out, "Do you know anything about my husband?" But I waited—afraid he did have news and that it wasn't good.

Finally he said, "My name is Mark Ogletree. My wife, Natalie, was in the building with your husband, and she was praying with him. She's been trying to contact you, but the phone lines have been jammed. She finally reached me and asked me to contact you."

I held my breath for the news.

"Mel," Mark continued, "your husband is on his way to Georgetown Hospital, and he's alive."

All of a sudden I felt as if God had turned my mourning into dancing, just as Psalm 30:11 talks about. The black cloud that had hung over me since I'd heard the Pentagon was hit had lifted. Brian was alive. I knew everything was going to be fine from that point on. Our lives would be back to normal.

I didn't know at that moment what Pollyannaish thinking that was. I had no clue, no clue whatsoever, what kind of situation I was walking into.

THREE

The Lone Casualty at Georgetown

★*Mel*

I hung up the phone just as my friend Debbie arrived. Matt was returning from his walk as Debbie got there, so they entered the house together.

"Brian's alive!" I yelled. "I just received a phone call that he's being rushed to Georgetown University Hospital." We were so excited, we were yelling and jumping up and down.

I grabbed the phone book, looked up the number for Georgetown, and called the emergency room. "My name is Mel Birdwell," I said as soon as a nurse answered the phone. "I understand Lieutenant Colonel Birdwell has been brought to the emergency—"

"Yes, ma'am. Just a moment." The nurse cut me off. "Let me get the attending physician for you."

Within moments Dr. Michael Williams, the trauma surgeon, was on the phone. "Mrs. Birdwell. Yes, your husband is here, and he is alive. But he is very severely injured. He is badly burned, and he has a severe inhalation injury."

Dr. Williams's words meant nothing to me. At least not at that time when I was merely focusing on the fact that Brian was alive and the rest of it was all going to be fine.

"Mrs. Birdwell, you need to get here as quickly as you can," Dr. Williams continued.

"Yes, of course. I'm leaving now," I told him.

I hung up the phone and tried to figure out just how I was going to get there. I knew I couldn't drive myself. For one thing, I had no clue where Georgetown was. For another, I knew I was not in any kind of mental condition to drive myself. If I drove, I figured I'd end up in the hospital right along with Brian—something we didn't need.

I knew I couldn't ask Debbie to drive me there because I really wanted her to stay with Matt. I didn't want Matt to go with me to the hospital because I had no idea what I would find when I arrived at Georgetown. I wasn't willing to expose my son, who was already dealing with his own intense emotions, to whatever I had to walk into. I certainly didn't want to have to worry about Matt as well as Brian.

So although I felt horribly guilty for not being able to be with Matt at such a difficult time for him, I asked Debbie to take care of Matt for me. She agreed immediately. Then I told Matt that Debbie was going to stay with him while I went to the hospital—that his dad had been severely injured. Matt seemed okay about not going. I think he was glad to know his dad was alive—but also afraid of seeing his dad in whatever condition he was in.

That was one of the hardest things for me to do, as a mom: to show my child through my actions, *I've got to choose your dad over you right now.* Even though I knew Matt understood why he wasn't going with me, I felt guilty leaving him behind.

The phone rang again. It was Major John Collison. I didn't know who he was, so he introduced himself as a coworker of Brian's. Then he told me he rode with Brian over to Georgetown Hospital. He said Brian was okay. And that when the nurse took off Brian's ring, Brian asked him to give it to me.

I thanked him, glad to hear from a friend who had been there with Brian. I hung up and began to think through my options for transportation to the hospital. Then the phone rang yet again. This time it was Judith Rogers, a nurse from Georgetown. "Mrs. Birdwell, are you coming?"

I thought it was odd that she called so soon after I'd hung up with Dr. Williams. But I merely said, "I'm working as fast as I can to get there."

"You've got to get here *now,*" she insisted. "He is very, *very* serious."

I swallowed hard, terrified by her voice. "Okay. I'll be there as quickly as I can."

That was probably the first really scary thing I understood. While Dr. Williams had said Brian was serious, I never imagined it was *deathly* serious. The doctor had just said to get there when I could. But then the nurse had phoned. . . .

I ran out of the house—I hadn't taken a shower, brushed my teeth, or put on makeup yet that morning. I didn't even bother to put on my shoes! I rushed to my neighbor Sara's house to ask her husband to take me to the hospital. I couldn't ask Sara because she was pregnant and was due in about nine more days.

When I got to Sara's, she told me her husband, Stu, wasn't home yet from work because the traffic was in a gridlock all over the city.

As I left her house, I wondered, *What am I going to do?*

Then, as I faced the opposite sidewalk I saw a soldier in a green camouflage uniform standing at the end of the street and talking on his cell phone. While I knew he and his family lived down there, I hadn't met them yet. I ran to him and explained the situation. "My name is Mel. My husband, Brian, was badly injured at the Pentagon. They've taken him to Georgetown Hospital, and I have to get there. But I don't know how to. Could you drive me?"

The neighbor introduced himself as John Miller, an Army sergeant major, and then said, "I don't know how to get to Georgetown either, but yes, I will drive you. Go back to your house and put on your shoes, then meet me here. We'll get you to Georgetown. Okay?"

I said okay and ran back to my house to fetch my shoes and to tell Matt I was leaving and would be back home that night. Then I asked Debbie, "Will you take him?"

"Absolutely. Don't worry about it. I'll take Matt home with me." Then she turned to Matt and suggested, "Why don't you get a change of clothes, so if you're at my house overnight you'll be set for tomorrow? We'll take your school stuff with us in case you need to stay longer."

When I tried to explain to Matt what was happening, he cut me off. "That's okay, Mom. I understand."

I put on my shoes, grabbed my purse and my cell phone, and ran out the door.

My neighbor John didn't have a map of the area, so I ran *back* to my house, grabbed a map, and rushed out.

I was eager and anxious to get there. But we needed to stop and get gas before we could start for Georgetown. I could hear the clock ticking down in my mind.

The only thing I did know about getting to Georgetown was that we needed to take Route 66. John was driving up Route 1. I kept thinking, *Oh my goodness, why is he going this way?*

Fortunately John knew what he was doing because this route ended up being the way with the least traffic. On a normal day, going to Georgetown from our house would probably take about half an hour.

But on September 11 it took us two hours. The entire time we were listening to the radio to hear if any other terrorist action was taking place, or if there was any other news. There was so much misinformation—car bombs exploding, mass chaos, possible bombs throughout the DC area set to detonate.

What is going on? I kept wondering.

When we arrived at the intersection of Route 1 and Interstate 495, where you normally can see the DC skyline, all I could see was the black smoke pouring from the Pentagon. I turned my head away. It was too much of a nightmare.

We kept listening to the radio as the news reporters announced the number of injuries and how many people had been taken to the different hospitals. I pricked up my ears when I heard them announce, "Georgetown University Hospital. One." *One?* I thought. *No way, that can't be right. There's no way there's just one person there.*

Panic set in. I wondered if Brian had died before I'd gotten there, so he wasn't counted in the totals. Horrible thoughts raged in my brain—and no matter how hard I tried, I couldn't control them. So I prayed. I silently willed every car to get out of our way. And I phoned Georgetown University Hospital every five minutes.

"How is he doing?" I'd ask.

They'd tell me the same things: "He's okay. He's intubated. He's sedated. He's fine."

Yet Judith's phone call made me not trust what the others were telling me. I was nervous, scared, and not very talkative. I just needed John to drive as quickly as he could. But the traffic was horrendous. It was as though we were sitting in a parking lot, the traffic was so gridlocked. There were several times I wanted to get out of the truck and start screaming, "Move it, people! My husband's been hurt. Why aren't you driving faster?" I wondered how they could be so passive when my world was falling apart.

Instead I prayed. *Please, Lord, keep him alive. I realize what that nurse said, but please don't let it be too serious.*

I kept telling myself, *He's just going to be in the hospital a few days, and then he'll be home and it will all be fine again.*

But I also knew the reality: I had no idea what I'd be walking into at Georgetown. And for me, that was the worst. I'm a master control freak, and I had no control over this situation.

I kept calling my house to check the answering machine because I knew Brian's family was going to call, and I'd not had the presence of mind to give them my cell phone number.

Finally, after two long hours, we made it to the Francis Scott Key Bridge—the bridge that connects Virginia and Washington DC. It's the way to Georgetown from Virginia. It would have been the same bridge Brian took to get to the hospital from the Pentagon.

Just as we arrived at the bridge, we encountered another huge traffic backup. Cars were lined up on Route 66 on the exit ramp to the bridge.

"What is taking so long?" I wondered aloud. We moved maybe a quarter of a mile in ten or fifteen minutes. I thought, *I can't do this anymore.*

We finally reached a place where we could see that the authorities were not letting any traffic into DC They were allowing cars to cross out of DC and into Virginia but not the other way—which was the way I had to go. So I turned to John and said, "I'm just going to get out and run the rest of the way. Thanks for bringing me. I'll worry later about how I'm going to get home tonight."

I hopped out of his truck and took off running toward the entrance of the bridge, where a police officer was directing traffic and keeping cars from crossing. I went straight up to him and explained, "My husband was injured at the Pentagon, and he's at Georgetown. I don't know how to get there from here."

"Cross the bridge," he said. "There's a police officer at the other end. Get him to call a DC police car for you, and he'll take you the rest of the way." I said okay and took off running again.

I'm not a strong runner, so trying to get there quickly was a challenge.

Plus I was crying, so it was hard to breathe. I ended up having to stop halfway across the bridge because I thought I was going to have a heart attack. The bridge is about a quarter of a mile across, but it seemed like fifteen miles across to me.

At that point I was so irrational that my mind started playing tricks on me. I started to freak out. *I'm going to die on Key Bridge, trying to get to the hospital, and Matthew's not going to have either parent. We're both going to die, and he's going to have nobody.* While I was clasping my side and struggling to breathe, I turned toward the direction of the Pentagon. I could still see the thick plumes of black smoke rising in the midafternoon sky. I couldn't take it—I began shaking, hyperventilating, and screaming out in anguish. I took off running again, still in pain and sobbing the whole way as I darted against the flow of people exiting into Virginia.

Finally I made it across the bridge and found the police officer. I explained the situation to him. But he announced, "There's not a DC police officer available for me to call. You're going to have to walk the rest of the way."

"How do I get there?" I asked.

He very coldly and uncompassionately informed me, "You go up there." He pointed toward a long hill. "Follow the hospital signs."

So I took off again. As I passed a group of businessmen walking toward me, I stopped them and asked, "Do you know how far it is to Georgetown Hospital?" One of the men said, "Yes, it's about four miles up that way."

"No way!" I screamed out, horrified. "It *can't* be four miles!"

"It's four miles."

I started to sob uncontrollably again. I thought, *I am never, ever going to get there! This is just too overwhelming.*

Again I took off running as best I could, trying not to think about the cramp in my side or how my lungs felt as though they were going to explode. I kept praying, *God, please just give me somebody who can take me the rest of the way. Please send me somebody who knows how to get there.*

I made it about a quarter to half a mile—uphill—when a DC police officer passed me in his squad car. I start waving wildly at him, but he just kept going. "No! You can't keep driving past me!" I shouted. I was hot, out of breath, sweaty, achy. And now I was mad.

★ *Brian*

Having survived everything else I thought this ride to the hospital was going to kill me.

As soon as Jill yelled, "We're going to Georgetown," the enlisted Navy man said, "I know the way! Follow me." And he took off on his motorcycle, racing down roads and over median strips, dodging oncoming or stopped traffic, with us trying to keep up.

Fortunately I couldn't see out the windows. But I heard enough to make me scared. Jill was yelling directions. John was yelling instructions and paying attention to me, checking that I was okay. Occasionally he would say, "Hang on, Sir." *With what?* I thought. *And to what?* I had nothing I could hang on to or hang on with. I was lying on the back of a body board. And I was paying attention to my breathing and the pain. I had no sense of where we were. I just knew Georgetown Hospital was across the river, not that far, maybe four miles away, yet it seemed as if it was taking a long time to get there.

Jill was yelling, "Watch out!" or some similar instruction. I could tell she was concerned that the shock I was in would kill me.

"Major," she said to Collison, "I need you to keep him alert and talking. Talk to him."

So John told me, "Hey, Sir, I'm still here. Talk to me. Let me know you're okay."

"My legs hurt," I told him. Then I figured I might as well know how I was really doing, so I asked, "How bad does it look?"

"Sir, to me," he said, "you look like you have flash burns. Your hair is burned back, and your face is charred."

"Okay, well, it hurts," I told him. "It hurts really bad."

With the attack on the Pentagon and reports that the Capitol and the White House were also targets, everybody was trying to escape DC and drive into Virginia—which is where we were. So as we would encounter traffic jams, the Navy motorcyclist would lead us over sidewalks and through lawns. Captain Wineland crossed over medians and into the other side of traffic. The motorcyclist, then Wineland would beep their horns as we drove through intersections so no one would hit us.

We were all getting jostled around. Jill and John were trying hard to keep from falling over onto me. That was probably why everyone in the car was yelling; they must have thought they were going to die along with me.

We crossed Key Bridge, which hadn't closed yet. But once we crossed the bridge, to get to Georgetown, which is situated in the middle of a residential area, we had to drive down narrow residential streets, which meant making really sharp, hard turns. Every turn and jostle of the vehicle was excruciating for me.

Finally we arrived at the hospital, found the emergency room door, and pulled up. Immediately a team of disaster specialists, since the hospital was on disaster alert, was outside with a stretcher. They opened the side door to the Expedition. I'm not sure why they opened that door, unless they thought I was sitting up. They realized quickly I was in the back, so they ran to the back door, pulled out the body board, set it on the gurney, and moved me inside.

The first physician to reach me was Dr. John DeSimone, the director of the emergency room. He helped pull the backboard out of the Expedition. He was the upfront physician who was responsible for evaluating my injuries. He took one look at me and realized I needed major resuscitation, so he ordered the staff to wheel me immediately to room 6, the trauma room of the emergency unit.

The morphine must have taken effect by this time because I was no longer shaking, and I didn't feel as much pain.

They lifted the body board and placed me on the first bed closest to the doorway. Then I was surrounded by a sea of doctors in white lab coats and nurses in disaster-alert vests. The organized chaos began. Each person started a particular procedure on me. They were as organized as a battle drill.

The medical staff was primarily concerned about my airway; they needed to secure it so it didn't close off completely. They were also worried about the internal burns and pulmonary damage.

The temperature of the air I was breathing in the Pentagon had burned and damaged my lungs. I don't think I inhaled flames; otherwise I would have had burns inside my mouth, which I didn't have.

I overheard them talking about an inhalation injury. They were very concerned about my lungs filling with fluid. If my lungs filled with fluid, which they had already begun to do, and the air passages closed from the burns and inhalation injuries, I would die.

Just as you blister on the outside when you get burned, the same thing happens to your lungs when they are burned. Water from your body rushes to the burn site to heal it, which causes you to blister. My lungs were filling with fluid, and I was beginning to blister on the inside. Basically, I was drowning without ever being in water. So the medical staff was rushing to drain the liquid from my lungs. With that fluid going to my lungs, I was unable to process the oxygen.

Dr. Williams, the trauma surgeon, and other members of the team began basic resuscitation care, securing the airway, IV access, and beginning diagnostic tests.

The first thing was to intubate me and put me on a ventilator for my breathing. I could still taste the jet fuel. I couldn't smell it, but several staff members commented on how strong it was. A lot of people were talking back and forth, but I didn't understand most of it because they were using medical language.

Then they began fluid resuscitation. Due to my burns, all of my bodily fluids were sucked into the blood vessels to make up for the fluid I'd lost. So they set up another IV to start giving me a large amount of fluid right away. They knew if they got behind in my fluid, I could die because my organs would begin to shut down.

As they were evaluating me for other injuries because of the explosion, they discovered a lump on the back of my head. They decided to schedule a CAT scan to check for head trauma.

Dr. Williams, who was standing next to me, said, "Brian, I'm Dr. Williams. I'm the trauma surgeon. You're hurt badly, but we're going to take care of you. We have to put you under anesthesia soon because we need to take you to surgery."

When he said, "put you under," I knew what that meant for me. I knew there was a serious possibility that if they anesthetized me, I might never come out. I knew I might be speaking my last words.

That was the most difficult moment for me up to this point. When the blast hit the Pentagon, that tough moment of dying was thrown upon me. But this moment lying in the emergency room at Georgetown wasn't. In a way I had known this moment was coming. I was badly injured; to take care of my wounds completely, I'd have to be anesthetized. So I'd had an opportunity to think about this moment on that trip to Georgetown.

I realized what I did and said right then may be my last words and actions, my last living act, so I wanted to make them count.

"Wait," I told Dr. Williams. "I need to do two things first."

I asked for the hospital's chaplain. Then I could see John Collison standing behind Dr. Williams, so I called for him to come to me. I asked him to take off my wedding ring. Because my skin was burned so badly, a nurse, Judith Rogers, had to do it. Some of the skin came off with the ring. Then Judith handed the ring to John.

"John," I said, "you make sure my wife gets this ring."

"Yes, Sir, I will," he said.

I knew there wasn't much time. While I wanted to talk with Mel, to hear her voice one last time, I knew calling her would have prolonged the trauma, and we were out of time. So I made my peace with her when I gave John the wedding ring to pass to her.

"Tell Mel . . . ," I started and choked back a cry. "Tell her . . . that I always loved her."

★ *Mel*

I continued to walk—and run whenever I could. I focused only on the next step my feet were taking because I couldn't look up at the twisting, winding hill I had to trudge up to get to my husband. Then my trek would seem impossible.

Thankfully, the police officer had seen me waving wildly, so he turned around and came back. I looked into the full car of four police officers and thought, *Great! If you four weren't in one car, there would be somebody available to take me to the hospital.* I knew that wasn't a nice thought, but I was so angry. So yet again I explained the situation, and the police officers told me to get in. They would drive me to the hospital, which I found out wasn't four miles away. One of the officers said, "Why didn't you call someone from your home, and they would have brought you in?" When I heard that, I couldn't help my anger and frustration. "I didn't know the Virginia State Police were an escort service."

He got the clue about my emotional state. He just said, "Okay."

I sat in the backseat of that squad car, sweaty and stinky because it was so hot that day. My face was blood red. All my emotions whirled, and I wept out loud from the stress—of trying to make it to Georgetown and not being able to, of not knowing how Brian was, of the guilt of not being with my son, to knowing I was finally going to make it to Georgetown and wondering what I'd find when I got there.

★*Brian*

Now that I'd passed my ring and my message to John, I was ready for the second important thing I needed to do: I needed to pray. *This is it,* I thought. *This will be the last prayer I ever pray.*

Okay Lord, I know this is not a mission you gave me, but you allowed me to receive it. If you will it, guide Dr. Williams's hand as he does what he has to do to me so I can live. And if not, then call me home from this operating room table so that the manner of my death will be a witness to your grace in my life.

Chaplain Linda Cirillo and I prayed, acknowledging God's sovereignty. And as we prayed I felt the presence of God so strongly it was almost tangible.

After the prayer I looked at Dr. Williams and said, "Okay, I'm ready. Let's get on with it." Dr. Williams directed someone to administer the anesthesia. A woman gently placed a mask over my face and carefully adjusted the head straps around my singed ears. She told me just to breathe. That was the last thing I remember.

★*Mel*

Unbeknownst to me, while I was in the backseat sobbing, one of the officers sitting up front called the hospital to let them know I was almost there. Moments later the police car pulled up to the Georgetown emergency room entrance and dropped me off. I quickly wiped my eyes and face with my hands, thanked the officers, then stumbled out of the car. There at the door stood a physician and Judith Rogers, the nurse who had called me more than two hours earlier.

"Mrs. Birdwell?" Judith said.

"Yes."

"Let's take you in to see your husband. He's in ICU. We have to go upstairs to get there. Let me try to prepare you for what you're going to see when you see him."

"Okay."

"But first, I need to tell you, your husband loves you. He was conscious until we sedated him, but he asked me many times to tell you he loves you. Actually, he *insisted* we tell you that," she said. "Now, he will look nothing like he looked this morning when he left your house. He is very badly burned and very, very swollen."

They had already told me this on the phone. But every time they told me, it didn't register because I'd never dealt with a burn before. I really knew nothing; I couldn't even tell you which was worse—a first- or third-degree burn. So as she told me he was burned, that truly was just a word to me. *He's burned. Okay. What does that mean?* I thought.

She said, "We've already debrided him a little."

That word *debrided* also meant nothing to me.

She continued, "He is sedated. He has a tube down his throat. And it's going to be very frightening to you when you go in."

Fine. I was just glad I had finally made it to the hospital and Brian was alive. Nothing else made any sense to me.

As we got to the ICU on the fourth floor, C 4-3, Judith stopped walking and turned to look at me. "Is there anything you need before you go in there?"

"Yes. I'd like to go to the bathroom and throw some cold water on my face." I knew my face had to be bright red because I was so hot. And I needed to regroup and pull myself together before I saw Brian.

Judith continued, "He's not going to know you're there since he's sedated. And you'll only be able to see him for just a few moments because we have to keep this as sterile an environment as possible."

She directed me to a public restroom down the hall from the ICU. I went in and stood for a moment. I stared in the mirror at my bloodshot, puffy eyes, my oversized and damp T-shirt, my messy hair, and red face. My eyes started to fill again as I grabbed the side of the sink. *God, I need your strength to get through this,* I prayed. I took a deep breath, turned on the faucet, and stuck my fingers under the water as I waited for it to get cold. Then I bent over the sink and splashed the cold water on my face.

I grabbed a paper towel and dabbed my face. Then I took one more look in the mirror. *I look horrible,* I thought. Then I stepped into the brightly lit corridor of the hospital ICU unit.

Judith was waiting for me. "Okay," she said gently, putting her arm around me, "let's go." As we walked she explained that a burn/trauma specialist resident and a burn staff nurse, who both had recently transferred from the Burn Unit at Washington Hospital Center, were working on Brian. The nurse, Debi Trichel, was washing him down to remove the remaining traces of jet fuel that were on him, as well as making sure his head was propped up to reduce the swelling since that would further challenge his airway. She had also finished removing the dead skin, with scissors, and was redressing him with new bandages.

We walked into ICU and around the nurses' main desk, toward the back of the unit to Room 12.

Dr. Williams and Dr. Clark, another attending physician, came to introduce themselves to me. They told me they had found a bump on the back of Brian's head and were worried about a concussion or a possible brain injury, so they had just given Brian a CAT scan.

Minutes clicked by like hours. I was desperate to see him—but also anxious.

A lot of people came up to advise me, but everything was just blurry to me. I was so overwhelmed with all the people around and everything that was happening. All these people kept saying, "This is what's happening. This is what the plan is. This is what we're doing."

Finally Judith said, "Are you ready to go in and see him?"

"Yes!"

She explained that more than 60 percent of Brian's body had been burned—and that almost 40 percent of the burns were third degree.

Then she told me that they have to take care of the burns immediately because degree burns continue to burn—so consequently, a second-degree burn can turn into a third-degree burn. They had cleaned up Brian—bathed him, cut away some of the burned tissue, and dressed him in bandages.

Judith handed me gloves, a gown, a hat, a mask, and shoes—everything sterile—and helped me put them on.

Then she led me to room 12.

There were people everywhere. As I walked into that dimly lit room and then over to the left side of the bed, I saw a figure lying there. But there was nothing about that figure that resembled my husband. Nothing. He was so incredibly swollen, his head was almost as wide as his shoulders. And he was white, so white his forehead was almost transparent. They had already scrubbed some of the skin off his face and put salve on him. But he just looked transparent. It was the whitest white I had ever seen in my life.

He still had hair, but it was pretty singed. There was a tube down his throat, and he was covered in bandages. Everything was bandaged.

I drew in my breath. *God, is this real?* I half prayed, half thought. *Is this really happening?* I was scared; it was so horrible. And Brian couldn't say anything to me since he was sedated; he didn't even know I was there.

I had prayed for Brian to be okay. But seeing him like this, okay seemed far from the Pollyanna thinking I'd had earlier. What would lie ahead of us?

I wasn't in the room that long because I couldn't handle seeing Brian like that. Judith escorted me from the room. I sat down in a chair outside his room and started to cry again. I felt so overwhelmed. I had to tell myself, *Mel, you can deal with this. You're going to be fine. Brian is going to be fine.*

"Are you okay?" Judith asked.

I looked up at her and nodded slightly. "I guess I'm as okay as I can be. I didn't really know what to expect."

"We're going to medevac your husband to Washington Hospital Center. They have a burn unit that specializes in trauma."

"How can you fly him there? Isn't all airspace closed?" I asked, remembering what I'd heard from the radio on the way to the hospital.

Judith explained that they had requested the FAA to open air space to medevac him to the Washington Hospital Center. Yes, while the FAA had closed all air space, they gave Georgetown special permission to fly Brian across town.

"We're trying to get a DC police escort to take you over."

"Can I fly with him?" I asked.

"No, I'm afraid not."

A social worker, Glenda, approached me and said, "Let's go into a more private room outside the ICU." I think they weren't sure how I was doing so they wanted to limit my exposure to all the activity around Brian.

She took me down the hall to a small room that had a phone. "Do you need to make any phone calls?"

"Yes, I need to call my son and my family." She helped me settle in the room, then walked out and closed the door.

I called Matt at Debbie's and told him, "I've seen Dad and he's alive, and that's really all I know right now."

"Tell Dad I love him," Matt said.

"Okay, I'll do that." I couldn't tell Matt how bad everything was.

Then I called Brian's mom and his brother, Wade.

At that point a different physician knocked on the door and stepped in. "Mrs. Birdwell, I'm Dr. Plotkin. We have the results on Lieutenant Colonel Birdwell's CAT scan. I thought you might want to know it came back negative, which is good. Frankly, Mrs. Birdwell, I'm amazed that Brian has no broken bones—especially given the force of the explosion."

His words, just as everyone else's, really meant nothing to me. How much worse *could* it be? I'd just seen a figure who looked nothing like my husband, but *was* my husband. How could the man who had happily kissed me good-bye in the morning now look like some swollen mess?

I thanked Dr. Plotkin for the news, then phoned my sister, Connie. "I don't know how I'm going to do this," I wept into the phone. "You should see him, Connie. It's awful."

Just then my cell phone rang. It was Steve Ener, Brian's best friend from high school and college. I told him what I knew.

Another social worker, Mary, came into the room and asked, "What can we do for you? What do you need?"

"I want a Bible." I hadn't brought my Bible with me because I didn't think I would need it. Now I realized how badly I *did* need it.

She left and a few moments later a Catholic priest entered. "Mrs. Birdwell, I'm going to find you a New Testament."

"No, I want a full Bible," I said.

"Why?" he asked, puzzled.

"Because I like the stuff in the Old Testament, too," I answered quickly.

When the priest left to find a full Bible, Glenda returned. "Mrs. Birdwell, you mentioned you haven't had a shower or brushed your teeth, so I thought you might want this. Here's toothpaste and a toothbrush for you. And here's twenty dollars. This is all the money I have with me. You're going to need some money because you're going to be at the hospital for quite a while."

I couldn't believe it—yet I was so grateful. When I'd left my house, I had only two dollars and my checkbook. I never carry cash in my wallet, and I didn't have an ATM card.

I immediately left to brush my teeth. Even that simple task made me feel so much better. What really made me calmer was when the priest brought me the Bible. I clutched it like I was holding onto a life raft in the middle of a raging ocean.

Afterward I returned to that private room and waited for them to find my transportation to the Washington Hospital Center. Mary and Glenda kept making phone calls to the DC police but were told, "We can't take her over there."

Finally the hospital administrator, along with the chief of security, William Cody, found out what was happening and intervened. William told the social workers, "Stop making phone calls. We're taking her over." He arranged for one of his security people to drive me to the hospital.

By mid to late afternoon, after Brian had been at Georgetown four or five hours, and I'd been there a little less than an hour, one of the nurses came to the room and said, "We're getting Brian ready to transport. You go on ahead so you can be there when he arrives."

The staff transported Brian to the hospital's helipad, which was outside the hospital by Georgetown University's football field.

The security guard escorted me to his car and we left. The drive was especially eerie. We watched as armed Humvees and other military vehicles sat on most corners of DC. Everywhere I looked, National Guard soldiers were holding M-16s.

I am in Washington DC, and this is like martial law, I thought. It was a very surreal drive down what were once normal streets. But there was no normalcy that day.

FOUR

The Transfer

★*Mel*

Finally, between four and five o'clock, after what seemed like hours, I arrived at Washington Hospital Center, where Brian was being medevaced. Hospital security personnel surrounded the emergency room entrance. I couldn't believe how much security I had to go through just to get into the building. It might as well have been Fort Knox!

They weren't allowing anyone through the doors since the hospital was on disaster alert, Code Orange. The scene was chaotic.

As soon as the plane hit the Pentagon, the hospital expected to have thousands of casualties. So they discharged everyone who wasn't in a life-threatening situation, sent every visitor out of the hospital, and called in every available staff person. That meant anyone who wanted to get into the hospital had to have a very specific reason.

I walked over to a man at the door who seemed to be in charge and explained, "My husband, Lieutenant Colonel Brian Birdwell, is being brought over from Georgetown Hospital."

He glanced through a listing, then dismissed me with, "We don't have anybody by the name of Brian Birdwell here, and we're not expecting anybody by the name Brian Birdwell."

"Look again harder!" I said and again explained the situation.

He must have realized I was about to become hysterical, so he stepped inside the emergency room to check, then returned. "There's nobody."

"He's on a helicopter, and he is on his way here!"

"Ma'am, calm down."

"I am not calming down! You have to find my husband!"

Again he walked quickly back inside. A few minutes later another person appeared and calmly said, "The helicopter has just arrived. Your husband will be in momentarily. So let's take you inside."

Honestly, though, I think at that point, if Brian's helicopter *hadn't* arrived, the staff were ready to make up a helicopter just to calm me down! They spoke to me in a patronizing, appeasing tone, as if to say, "We're taking you to a nice, quiet rubber room."

I didn't care; I'd had enough.

A hospital staff member escorted me to the hospital's lobby. There they were processing victims' family members to update them and tell them where they needed to go. Since Brian hadn't officially been admitted yet, the processing people instructed me to sit and wait until someone had more information.

I waited about five minutes, then was called to the desk to explain again Brian's circumstance. I repeated that he'd been medevaced in from Georgetown Hospital. Finally they understood that he was a serious casualty. So they found someone to escort me up to the Burn Unit ICU on 4H, the fourth floor, to meet with another social worker.

The halls were eerily quiet. I kept thinking how surreal this seemed. This morning Matt and I were having fun working on a science experiment; we were so excited about showing Brian when he got home from work. Now I was walking along a hospital corridor, wondering if Brian would ever see that experiment—or worse, if Brian would ever see me.

My escort stopped in front of a small waiting room. Since the social worker was talking with another victim's family, the escort asked me to wait outside, then she left.

Now what am I supposed to do? I wondered as I stood alone in the hallway. I had no idea what to expect, what to do, or what to think. As I waited, I stared down the sterile, white fluorescent-lit hallways. They reminded me a little of Brian's hallway at the Pentagon—not that I wanted to make that comparison.

After about five or ten minutes, the door opened and two women stepped into the hallway. One of them looked pale and stunned. The other woman looked at me and said, "Are you Mrs. Birdwell?"

"Yes."

"I'm Nancy Fox, the social worker. Come in and we can talk."

As soon as I entered the room, Nancy closed the door and sat in a chair across from me. Her face registered no emotion. She looked businesslike and detached, which made me feel uncomfortable and a little irritated, especially with everything that had happened in the last few hours. Then she started into a matter-of-fact speech: "Your husband is currently being evaluated by burn center staff. He's going to be in the hospital for a while. There's a hotel in the hospital, and it's ninety dollars a night. You'll need to go there and get a room. I'll have one of the chaplain's assistants take you over. Or I can tell you how to get there, and you can find it on your own."

Then she stopped talking and simply waited for me to say something.

"Somebody will need to take me because I'll never find it on my own," I finally said.

"Fine. As soon as we know anything, we'll let you know."

And that was it. The conversation was over. She stepped over to the door, opened it, and waited for me to leave. No words of sympathy or comfort. No looks of concern. Nothing. I was "just another family member." I thought, *Well, thank you very much. You were completely not helpful.*

So back out into the hallway I went and waited for the chaplain's assistant to arrive. Fortunately I didn't have to wait long.

"Do we have to go there right now?" I asked the chaplain's assistant. "I really want to be near Brian."

"It's going to be awhile before you can see him," she said. "They took him immediately from the helicopter into intensive care. They're doing an assessment. Since that's going to take some time, we might as well go ahead and book your hotel room."

We walked along a labyrinth of corridors with their twists and turns. There was a diamond-shaped pattern on the floor, so I focused on following it to remember where I was going and how to get back to the ICU. Meanwhile I kept thinking, *Ninety bucks a night? How long can we afford ninety dollars a night? Not long at all, that's for sure. Where are we going to get the money for this?*

We arrived at the hotel registration desk. I was still wondering how I was going to afford the room. Finally I decided just to go ahead and do it, not worry about it, and figure it out later. But as I pulled out my checkbook, I thought, *Oh, Brian, I should have listened more to you when you told me about money issues!*

After I secured the hotel room, I returned to the ICU. It was about a five-minute walk, although—just like everything else—it seemed like a five-hour walk.

As I entered the waiting room, I saw the woman I had seen earlier with Nancy Fox. She looked as empty as I felt.

I went over to her, and we started to talk. I found out her name was Veronica Cruz, and she told me a little more about her husband, Juan. Apparently Juan had been critically burned—not by the fire, but by the heat. The heat had become so intense in his office that it cooked about 70 percent of his body with third-degree burns.

I hugged her and told her how sorry I was to hear about her husband. She thanked me. Then everything felt awkward. Neither of us knew what to do. So we simply sat next to each other, not saying anything, nervously awaiting word about our husbands.

All I could do was pray.

My cell phone began to ring, mostly from family members I'd given my number to on the way to the hospital. Since Brian, Matt, and I had moved to Virginia specifically for his Pentagon assignment, most of our family was out of state in Texas, Kansas, California, and Oklahoma. Understandably they were concerned and wanted to make the long trip by car. I told them they didn't need to come at this time. I really didn't know anything else about Brian's condition yet—not to mention it was still chaotic driving around the city.

The halls were filling with other victims' family members. No one interacted initially because all of us were so involved in our own thoughts, our own worlds, our own families. We didn't have the emotional or physical energy for anything else.

But I did notice I was the only person who was alone.

A husband and wife must also have noticed because they approached me.

"I'm Eloise Clarke, and this is my husband, Charles. Our daughter, Antoinette Sherman, was in the Pentagon. Was your husband hurt there, too?"

"Yes, my husband, Brian."

"Our pastor is here, and he's going to pray with our family. Why don't you join us, and we'll pray for your husband, too?"

I felt so loved when the Clarkes did that. Antoinette's family latched onto me and took me in as one of their own. There must have been at least twenty members of her family there, plus her pastor. Every time they prayed together, they had me join them. And they prayed for Brian every time. To hold hands in that circle and have people lifting up a total stranger to the Lord is the most comforting, wonderful feeling. I don't know what I would have done without them during that horrible period of waiting.

Around 7 P.M. Nancy Fox, the social worker, approached me with a piece of paper. I glanced at the paper; it had the name of a social worker and a phone number written on it. I looked up at Nancy for more information since his name wasn't familiar to me.

"You're to call him," she stated, again in a matter-of-fact tone. "He's from Walter Reed Medical Center and needs to talk to you."

Great, I thought. *This is the last thing I want to do. I don't know this person, I'm not interested in talking to another social worker, and I'm not calling him.* So I folded the paper and stuck it in my purse, determined to blow it off. I had an uneasy, unsettling feeling. For some reason I couldn't explain, I felt that if Walter Reed Army Medical Center (WRAMC), the Army's hub medical center, was calling me, it wasn't for something good. I knew the Army would get involved in Brian's medical care; I was resistant to that happening because I knew Walter Reed didn't have burn specialists. I wanted Brian to receive the best possible care. That was at Washington Hospital Center, where they specialized in treating burns.

I felt overwhelmed and out of control; nausea was my constant companion. I was afraid Walter Reed was going to handle this situation in what I felt was their stereotypical military form: Give him some Motrin, and he'll get better. I figured they would treat him in an okay-he's-done-next-person fashion, as if he were a throwaway soldier. And I was not going to have that. That wasn't going to happen to my husband.

The other families and I remained in the waiting area, sitting quietly. None of us really knew anything. But we did know this: Of everyone injured at the Pentagon, the worst of the injured were in this ICU, right across from where we were now seated. And the worst numbered seven. And Brian was among the seven.

★ ★ ★

Around 11:00 P.M. Nancy approached me again. This time she handed me a thick stack of faxed paperwork.

"You need to sign this so they can medically retire your husband."

"What? I'm not signing this. I'm not medically retiring Brian."

"Well, then you need to call the social worker at Walter Reed."

Medically retire Brian? What are they saying? I thought. Then it hit me. *They think Brian is going to die! Do they know something no one has told me?* I wondered, suddenly shaky and very anxious.

Nancy said, "Come into the nurse's lounge. We'll sit down and talk about this, and you can use the phone in there."

I followed her into the lounge in the ICU and phoned the number on the fax.

The social worker answered, and as soon as I said who I was, he told me that Brian's death was imminent within seventy-two hours.

The Army had prepared the paperwork I was holding to begin processing Brian's medical retirement. I needed to sign the paperwork as soon as possible, preferably tonight. He explained that medically retiring Brian *before he died* would be financially beneficial to me *when* he died.

I became angry with him and everybody else at Walter Reed. *How do they know Brian is going to die?* I thought. *They haven't seen him. They don't completely know his condition.*

I also knew they weren't God. And I believed God could do anything—even heal my husband and keep him from dying.

So I said, "I don't believe Brian's death is imminent as you say. And how can you assess that from where you are since you haven't been here to see him?"

"Dr. Jordan told us his death was imminent."

"Then I'm going to talk to Dr. Jordan because I don't agree that his death is imminent."

"Mrs. Birdwell, these are your options. You can medically retire Colonel Birdwell now and receive 75 percent of his base pay for the rest of your life. If you wait and he dies before you sign the paperwork, your benefits will greatly decrease—you'll receive only a one-time life-insurance payment. Mrs. Birdwell, our intent is to provide the best outcome for you and your family. If you medically retire him and he survives, he can go through a board process in eighteen months and then he can return to active duty. The time he's medically retired, however, won't count toward his service time."

The social worker went on and on, throwing a lot of information at me very quickly. I was having trouble understanding and making sense of it all. *He's not even speaking English! What is he saying to me?*

Finally, I said, "Whoa, let's just stop right here. None of this makes sense. I'm going to call a friend of mine who will understand what you're saying. I'll have her call you and figure this out."

"Mrs. Birdwell," he said firmly, "I'd strongly advise you not to wait. You don't want to be left with no financial support when your husband dies."

I hung up the phone and tried to calm down. Maybe I was in denial, but I wanted desperately to believe my husband was going to survive. I looked at Nancy, who was standing nearby. "Nancy, you need to find Dr. Jordan for me because I need to talk to him *now.*"

At that moment Dr. James Jeng, Brian's primary burn surgeon, entered the lounge, sat at a table, and began to eat some Doritos. He'd just come from surgery.

I explained the situation to him. Dr. Jeng, I found out, was a Reserve Navy Commander (the Navy's equivalent to the Army's Lieutenant Colonel), so he was familiar with military policies and procedures.

"Who are you?" he asked.

"Mel Birdwell."

"Colonel Birdwell is your husband?"

"Yes."

"Well, Mrs. Birdwell, I think his chances of survival are 60/40, maybe 65/35. You need to get on that phone," he said as he nodded toward a phone in the room, "and ask some tough questions before you make any decisions."

"I don't know what tough questions to ask."

"You need to figure that out."

Thank you so very much, I thought. *You people are just a world of help to me. I have no idea what to ask!*

I left the room feeling overwhelmed, confused, and very alone. How could I make such a huge decision? Decisions about soldiering and retirement were my husband's realm, not mine.

I had called the shots before about other issues during our fifteen-year marriage—when Brian was deployed during Desert Storm and in 1999 for hurricane relief in El Salvador. Making choices without the ability to consult the husband is normal for an Army wife. But this decision was bigger, more important—this affected his entire future.

I found Nancy and told her, "Please find Dr. Jordan. I have to talk with him." Dr. Marion Jordan was Director of the Burn Center.

While I waited for Dr. Jordan, I began to pray for wisdom. *God, show me what I should do.*

Instantly I felt the Lord impress upon me, *Do not retire him.*

I knew medical retirement would be the last thing in the world Brian would ever want. He's a soldier through and through; he loves it more than anything he's ever done in his life. And I felt in my heart that he wasn't going to die, that he was going to get better, regardless of what that social worker and everyone else over at Walter Reed said. I didn't want to have to go into Brian's room in two or three weeks and say, "Guess what? I medically retired you. Get well soon."

What kind of motivation to get better would that be for somebody who loved being a soldier? To tell him, "You're not a soldier anymore"? That would crush him. I could not do that to him. A terrorist flies a plane into your building, and you're the one who has to pay the price with your career? That's just wrong.

My decision was made: no.

So I called Karen Foley, our financial advisor, and asked her to call the social worker at Walter Reed to help me sort out all the information he had thrown at me, then to let me know what it all meant. "And Karen," I said, "I don't care what he says about medical retirement. I am not medically retiring Brian."

"Okay, Mel," she answered. "I'll talk to him and find out what's going on. I'll put all this together, and call you back."

After another few moments, Dr. Jordan appeared.

"Dr. Jordan, I'm Mel Birdwell. The people at Walter Reed are telling me Brian's death is imminent and that I should medically retire him. Is that true? *Is* his death imminent?"

I was trying so hard not to cry. But as soon as I asked Dr. Jordan about Brian's death, I started to weep.

"No, Mrs. Birdwell," Dr. Jordan said compassionately. "I haven't informed anyone that Brian's death is imminent because I do not believe that to be the case. I don't give odds on survival chances. I'm not going to tell you 50/50 or whatever. However, I do not believe Brian is going to die. He has a long, hard road ahead of him, but I believe he's going to make it."

"Thank you," I said, relieved. "That's all I need."

That sealed it for me. No medical retirement.

"For what it's worth," he continued. "I wouldn't medically retire him either. Of course, that's your decision. I'm a former Navy man so I understand about the military. But it's not what I would do."

I thanked him again just as Karen called me back and began to lay out everything for me. I didn't understand what she was saying either!

"Whoa, Karen! You're speaking a language I don't understand. I'm too overwhelmed with everything going on right now. You're throwing too many dollar signs at me. Look, this is the bottom line: I'm not going to medically retire him. That's my decision, and that's what I'm sticking to."

"Okay, Mel. But you'll need to contact the social worker and let him know definitely."

So I called him at Walter Reed again and told him my decision.

"Mrs. Birdwell," he said crisply. "I think you're making a mistake."

"Well, that's my decision, and I'm sticking with it."

I hung up the phone thinking, *This is a dead issue. I don't have to deal with this again. Whew. That's one battle down.* I felt like I was being attacked because I'd had to make such a decision on the worst night of my life.

Then I decided to call home to get our messages. Once I called, though, I realized I didn't have anything to write on.

A friend of Antoinette's noticed I was searching for paper and pulled out a GMAC notebook from his pocket. "Would you like to have this?"

"Oh! Yes, I would. Thank you so much."

I was surprised to find our answering machine was full. We had more than thirty-five messages—and more than thirty of them were from the media.

How in the world did the media know about Brian? And how did they get our phone number? I wondered. I certainly didn't want to talk to the media.

The rest of the evening I spent pacing the halls outside the ICU. I stared at the parquetlike pattern on the floor for hours. I prayed, I talked on the phone to my sister or Brian's family, anything to make the time pass.

Sometime between 2 and 3 A.M. I was sitting on the floor in the hallway, praying, when an Army general walked past me.

After the medical retirement issue I dealt with earlier, I was a bit leery of anyone in uniform walking into ICU. So I always stopped them and asked if they were there to see Colonel Birdwell, since he was the only Army active-duty man there.

Since this was a three-star general, however, I tried to be a little gentler—since three-star generals are a little more powerful than the average colonel!

I stood and stopped him. "Excuse me, Sir. Are you here to see Colonel Birdwell?"

"Yes, I am. Are you Mel?"

"Yes, I am."

"Nice to meet you, Mel. I'm General Peake, Surgeon General of the Army. Have you seen Brian yet?"

"No, not here. I did see him at Georgetown, though."

"Let's go in and see Brian together."

Finally, after almost ten hours of waiting, I was able to see my husband.

I didn't think he could look worse than the last time I saw him. I was wrong. Brian was still swollen but not as badly as before—mostly because the surgeons had cut excisions to release the fluids that had built up around his burns, to keep his body from rupturing. They had cut open a majority of his body. Most of his body was bandaged, but the rest was horrific to see. No skin, bloody, cut, and oozing. And because of all the bandages, my normally thin husband looked huge.

Brian was heavily sedated and had no idea we were there, so we stayed only a few moments.

As we left, General Peake stopped me at the nurses' station. "How are you doing?"

"Well, pretty crappy, as a matter of fact," I answered truthfully. "This is horrible."

He nodded, then asked, "How's your son?"

"Not great either."

"Has he been here yet to see Brian?"

I shook my head.

"Well, you need to get him up here soon."

"That's not going to happen, Sir. This is not what he needs to see."

"You need to start thinking about getting Matthew up here, Mel. Now, is there anything the Army can do for you?"

"Well, Sir, a medical retirement issue came up tonight," I said, thinking he would tell me not to worry about it, that he'd set the people at Walter Reed straight.

Instead the general said, "You understand, the medical retirement issue will have to be looked at again."

That certainly wasn't the answer I wanted to hear.

"Sir, then I'd like an active-duty Army person to hold my hand through this. That way, the next time it comes up, I won't be caught off guard and will have a clue about what's going on."

I needed someone who was active-duty—someone whose job it was to be in the Army—because a full-time, hard-charging "green suiter" would completely understand what was going on and would give me the straight scoop.

General Peake nodded and said he would take care of that for me.

I couldn't help but wonder what would come of my request.

Then we walked out of the ICU. Back out in the hall, General Peake put his hand on my shoulder. "Mel, you need to try to get some food and sleep. You should get at least six hours of sleep a night. The colonel is going to need you to be healthy and strong."

Then he left.

But I didn't sleep. I spent the rest of the night waiting for Brian's various test results, watching CNN, and using that GMAC notebook to start a journal.

It would be the first of many sleepless nights.

FIVE

The Day After

JOURNAL 9/12/01
Got in to see Brian this morning. He is in tremendous pain.

★*Mel*

I spent that first night in the hallway and the waiting room by the ICU. I was able to sleep every so often for about fifteen minutes or so. Throughout the night the families received periodic updates from Drs. Jordan and Jeng and some of the nurses.

They told us that the first forty-eight hours after a burn injury are always the most critical. So the families waited with the knowledge that while their loved ones had survived the crash, they weren't out of the woods yet.

There were medical personnel everywhere. The hospital had called in every available staff person, including visiting nurses. Anybody who could possibly treat a burn wound was working twelve-hour shifts. And everyone seemed to be working on full adrenaline. Each person had a nurse assigned right outside his or her room. So Brian had a nurse who sat and looked at him the whole time. They stationed nurses for each patient around the clock.

Finally Kristi Montgomery, one of the ICU nurses, asked me if I wanted to see Brian. I jumped up. "Yes!"

Although he was still heavily sedated, I could tell he was in tremendous pain. And he hadn't opened his eyes up to this point.

Kristi was a wonderful nurse. She told me everything that was happening to Brian. She explained that when Brian first arrived the day before, they had evaluated his injuries, taken him directly into what's called *the tank* to debride him, then moved him into surgery for further debridement and excisioning.

"What's that?" I asked.

"Excisioning? Doctors Jordan and Jeng, the officiating physicians, cut Brian to keep him from exploding. This is normal procedure. Basically, the fluid builds in a burn victim's body, so the doctors need to cut where the most fluid gathers. They can drain it and begin to work."

I didn't say anything. *Cutting Brian to keep him from exploding?* The words rang in my head. I wasn't even sure now I wanted to know any more about excisioning.

We walked into room 6, Brian's room. It was filled with all these strange beeping and blinking machines to monitor every part of his body.

Kristi explained the importance of everything the medical staff did for a burn victim. They had to remove his burned skin as soon as possible so it wouldn't form a tourniquet. She told me how vital it was to keep Brian hydrated. As long as they could keep his cells hydrated, they could reduce the amount of tissue death. This is especially imperative since burns continue to burn, or deepen, if they aren't adequately hydrated.

They had to flush large amounts of fluids through his kidneys at a rapid rate or else his cells would continue to die, which would cause him to go into renal failure. In addition to watching the amount of fluids going into Brian's body, they had to monitor the amount of urine going out. Brian had to have an hourly minimum of 30 ccs of urine coming out to make sure the kidneys were still functioning and they were getting hydrated.

Because of all the fluid moving through Brian's body, the nurses had to monitor closely the amount of fluid that could build in his lungs, called *pulmonary edema,* which becomes a life-threatening problem because of the long-term involvement of all the hydration.

Brian had suffered an inhalation injury when his lungs were burned. So they had to drain liquid off his lungs because his body was rushing fluid to that part to heal it. Unfortunately, with the fluid moving to his lungs, he was unable to process oxygen.

I couldn't keep track of all the different types of fluids and medications. But I was impressed by how closely the nurses monitored Brian to make sure everything was in balance for his survival.

Before now I hadn't realized all the problems involved with critical burns. I always thought a burn was bad, but you put some salve on it, do some skin grafts, and it heals. I never thought about the effects burns have on all the organs of the body. The skin is the largest organ in the body, and it affects everything. So a burn is actually a multisystem injury. A burn affects every organ, the respiratory system, even the cardiac system. It changes a person's fluid status. The intercellular, extracellular fluids are affected. Plus burn injuries can cause muscle death. They can shut down a body.

While I had heard of first-, second-, and third-degree burns, I didn't realize there were also fourth-degree, which go through every layer of skin and reach the tissues and muscle, and fifth-degree burns, which go all the way down to the bone. Some of the victims had fourth and fifth-degree burns. Those patients had to have amputations. Brian was fortunate to keep all his limbs.

Kristi was patient as she explained what she was going to do next: "Let's see if he can do anything we tell him to do."

"Okay," I said, unsure of what she was going to tell him.

All of a sudden she said loudly, "Brian! I need you to wiggle your toes for me."

I looked down at his feet, the only part of him that wasn't burned or bandaged.

"Brian!" she said again, loudly. "Wiggle your toes."

Brian's toes began to wiggle a little.

Kristi and I looked at each other, our faces lighting up and showing huge smiles.

I was so excited I started to cry.

Brian, I knew you weren't going to die! I thought. *Those people at Walter Reed were wrong. I knew it!*

Kristi said, "Okay. Let's wait a little while and do it again." So we waited, and she asked him to wiggle his toes again. Sure enough, he did. We did the wiggle-your-toes bit several times. After that she said, "Talk to him all the time because if he can hear your voice and he knows you're here, that will help to keep him calm."

So I walked to the side of his bed and began to talk to him. He didn't turn his head toward me but kind of leaned it a little toward the side I was on. Again, I was delighted to know he wasn't going to die. How could he? He was responding to my voice.

I wasn't able to stay with him long because Kristi needed to do his dressing change, and she told me, "This is going to be very painful for him." So back out into the hall I went.

I decided to walk over to the hotel to be alone and spend some quiet time praying.

It was about 10 A.M. when I returned. Eloise, Antoinette's mother, came over to me and said, "There's some Army guy named Rota looking for you. He said he's a friend of yours."

Oh, great, now *what?* I thought. I had no idea who this person was, so I certainly wasn't going to go out of my way looking for him. I figured I'd resume my place in the waiting room, and if he found me, *then* I'd talk with him. Not five minutes later, here came this full colonel bounding into the room like a hurricane. He blew right over to me and took charge.

"Hey, Mel!" he said. "How are you doing? Good to see you."

"Who are you?" I blurted out.

Unfazed, he said, "Come on out to the hallway. I want to talk to you for a minute."

I must have hesitated because he said, "My name is Dane Rota. I work in the resource division in the office of ACSIM (Assistant Chief of Staff for Installation Management). Jan Menig and Major General Van Antwerp sent me here to help you." Jan Menig was Brian's boss, and the general was *the* boss over Brian's department.

"Are you the person I asked General Peake to send to help me?"

"Yes."

I was stunned, not sure I'd heard him correctly. I had never known the Army to work that quickly.

"But that was only about seven hours ago," I said.

"Yeah, the Army works fast, doesn't it?"

That's an understatement, I thought. Last night when I'd asked for an active-duty Army guy, I figured I'd never see anybody. And if I did, he'd show up, say, "Hey, what do you need?" then act like, "Okay, so I've done what was requested of me. Now let me go." I just couldn't believe they'd really sent someone—and a colonel at that.

We stood in the hallway and talked about the medical retirement issue and some other things, when Jan Menig and her husband, Bob, arrived.

"Hi, Mel," Ms. Menig said. "How are you?"

She gave me a brief hug, then handed me a bag. "I brought you some things."

I looked in the bag. It was filled with magazines and essentials, such as hair gel, Tylenol PM, and deodorant, which I was extremely thankful for, considering I hadn't yet taken a shower and was still in my clothes from yesterday morning.

Then she handed me some cash and said softly, "This is for you while you're here."

She began to tell me her own 9/11 story. Ms. Menig and General Van Antwerp worked in the same office area as Brian. Their windows also had flames shooting from them. Fortunately, though, they were in a hotel across the street from the Pentagon for a conference when the plane hit. She had spent most of the day trying to account for her staff and then trying to get home, and had not been able to get in touch with her husband. Meanwhile her husband had gone over to the area where her office was, thinking she was inside and dead.

"I'm glad I had that meeting," she said. "Otherwise, I *would* have been dead—especially since the plane crashed into the building right next to my office. When I finally made it home last night, I walked in and Bob started to sob. We just held each other."

It was an amazing story as she told it. I realized she must have been in shock, too, to come that close to death. And I could definitely understand what her husband had gone through.

"Can we go in to see Brian?" she asked.

We tried to get her in to see him, but the nurses wouldn't allow any visitors because they were changing his bandages. They stayed and visited with me for a while, making sure I was okay and asking if I needed anything. Then they left.

Dane turned to me and said, "Have you eaten anything yet this morning?"

I told him I hadn't—and wasn't interested in doing so. I hadn't eaten in two days.

"You have to eat," he said. As he began to usher me to the cafeteria, Sheila Little and Debbie Vance arrived—without Matt. I missed my son, but I knew he couldn't handle seeing his dad right then. Debbie assured me that Matt was okay and was welcome to stay with her family as long as he needed to. I called him right away and could hear the strain and struggle in his voice.

"Son, your dad's burned pretty badly, and he's in the ICU," I told Matt. "I saw him this morning, and he wiggled his toes, but I think he's going to be here awhile, which means I'm going to need to be here too. Do you understand?"

"Yeah, Mom, I understand." Then he paused. "Mom, I really miss you."

My heart ached. I tried to comfort and reassure him as much as I could. "We both love you very much," I told him. "Do you think you can hold on until Friday, just two more days, to spend some time with me?"

He said he could.

Dane kept pestering me to eat something, so finally we went to the cafeteria, where I picked out a small salad. I was able to eat only a few bites before I became nauseated. I didn't want to eat anyway; I wanted to go back to the ICU to be near Brian. I was uncomfortable being so far away—especially in case something happened.

We returned to the waiting room. Most of the day was spent updating visitors and others who called. I was able to see Brian periodically until the nurses kicked me out to do his wound care.

Some FBI agents showed up and wanted to know if I had any pieces of Brian's clothing from yesterday. I told them I didn't. They were extremely interested in retrieving anything they could since his clothing was considered evidence and was part of an official crime scene. Apparently, the agents also went to Georgetown and tried to retrieve his clothing there as well, but what hadn't been burned off his body had been cut off and thrown away.

Later that day a representative from the hospital came to the waiting room to talk with all the family members. He informed us that because of the significance of 9/11 and the injuries our family members had suffered, the hospital was going to hold a press conference. There would be only one—then they would ask the media to leave the families alone. The rep asked if anyone would volunteer to act as the family representative to answer any questions the press may have. Mike Kurtz, Louise's husband, volunteered.

Louise, an accountant, had just started working at the Pentagon a day before 9/11. That morning she went to a fax machine to send some files and was engulfed in a fire ball that burned her severely.

Even though I really didn't want anything to do with the media, I offered to go downstairs and sit with Mike for moral support, to be his cheerleader.

The hospital assured us this would be the only interaction we would have to have with the press.

Later, one of our pastors, Jack Elwood, came and offered comfort and prayed with me. He let me know that our church, Immanuel Bible Church, was going to hold a prayer vigil that night specifically for Brian.

Many friends and church members came by to offer their support, concern, and prayers. I felt so uplifted by those prayers and words of comfort. I'm not sure I would have made it through that day emotionally intact without them.

Debi Davis, a friend from our church, offered to pick me up on Friday to get Matt and spend the night with him at our house. I figured that would also give me a chance to get some paperwork together and to pack a few clothes. I had realized late last night that Brian always kept our bills at his desk in the Pentagon to pay them from there, which meant all our bills had burned. Somehow I needed to figure out which bills he had, how much we owed, and pay them.

Karen Foley also stopped by to offer support and explain some more financial information. Colonel Rota and Karen walked me through the financial aspect of medical retirement again. And again I told them both my decision had been made. No retirement. Period.

Dane Rota stuck by me every minute—sometimes so much that he drove me crazy! He was there too much! He was like my shadow. But even in those moments, I knew I desperately needed him with me. I'm not sure I could have made it through without him. But I felt bad because I couldn't get his name straight. My brain was so overwhelmed with the stress, I felt as if it was working at about one-third the capacity. So I kept calling him Rota Dane—and he kept saying, "It's Dane. Dane Rota." Then I'd have to say, "Sorry. I knew that."

I talked to Brian's family. They were still concerned and kept telling me they were praying for Brian and me. I told Brian's brother, Wade, that he and his family needed to come. He said they were on their way. It would be a few days before they could arrive, since they were coming by car from Texas. All airplanes were still grounded.

Again, I called on my friend Debi Davis and asked her to arrange for my house to be cleaned since Brian's family was going to stay there.

Then I called some long-time, close Army friends, the Boykins, and asked if they'd watch our dog, Hayley, while we stayed at the hospital.

Sometime in the afternoon the White House florist showed up in ICU with a huge cart of flower bouquets. She presented them to all the families on behalf of President and Mrs. Bush, explaining that the flowers had been cut from the Rose Garden that morning. They were beautiful. Across the cart hung a red, white, and blue ribbon with USA printed in the middle of it. All the family members cut the ribbon and then wore pieces of the ribbon on our clothing.

While all the visits and surprise flowers were nice, really all I wanted was to see Brian. I was in his room as often as they'd allow me.

Obeying Kristi's command to talk to Brian, I talked to him about everything that was happening, except for any details that might be upsetting, such as the medical retirement issue. I told him about everyone who visited or called. I talked about the other victims' family members and how kind they were.

I'd never have left his side, except the hospital staff made me leave at certain times. During those times the staff changed his dressings or put him in the tank—both excruciating experiences for Brian. Because of the nature of burns continuing to kill cells, the medical staff scheduled Brian to visit the tank every day to be debrided, getting rid of dead skin and tissue.

Later that evening Jack Elwood called to tell me that between thirteen hundred and fourteen hundred people attended the prayer vigil at church. And they spent a long time praying specifically for Brian. I hoped and trusted God would hear those prayers on behalf of my husband and everybody else who desperately needed a miracle.

When the nurses allowed me to return to Brian's room, I told Brian about all those people praying for him. Then I spent the rest of that night rubbing his feet—the one place I could touch without causing him tremendous pain. How grateful I was for even that small skin contact with the husband I loved so much. It was the only thing that seemed somewhat "normal" since the Pentagon was hit.

SIX

No Rest for the Weary

JOURNAL 9/13/01
*"He opened his beautiful green eyes this morning for the first time.
When I went in first thing . . . his eyes were opened. His eyes were just
wandering around the room, but when he saw me, he locked on me. It
was awesome. . . . God, Brian is in your hands and arms. Protect him—
and give Dr. Jeng a supernatural wisdom."*

★*Mel*

At about 7:30 A.M., on September 13, I was walking back from the hotel
room, where I'd gone to wash my face and try to freshen up, when my
cell phone rang. I thought that was odd, considering not too many people had my cell phone number. I looked at the phone number on my
caller ID. It read "Unknown Caller."

"Hello?"

"Mrs. Birdwell?"

"Yes?"

"This is the Secret Service. We're calling on behalf of the President.
He would like your permission to visit Colonel Birdwell today."

For just about the first time in my life, I was speechless.

"Mrs. Birdwell?"

"You're talking about the President—of the United States? President
Bush?"

"Yes, ma'am."

"How did you get my cell phone number?"

"Ma'am, we're the Secret Service."

"Oh!" I said, embarrassed. "Okay. Yes, the President can most definitely visit my husband." It was mind-boggling to think that the President would ask permission.

"Good. Thank you," the agent continued. "And Mrs. Birdwell, please don't discuss this with anyone. We need to keep this as quiet as we can."

"Okay."

Then he hung up.

The President was going to come, and I wasn't supposed to tell anyone?

I returned to the burn center and saw Secret Service everywhere. When I saw so many people who wouldn't normally be there, such as other hospital staff members I'd never seen before, I realized that somehow word must have leaked that the President was coming to the hospital that day. I mentioned it to Dane Rota, who told me that he found out the Secret Service had actually been there the day before, and not one of us had noticed all these Secret Service people combing the place, trying to figure out security issues and everything else that goes into bringing a President into an unsecured hospital. I was impressed because we were *very* tuned into who was coming and going through those halls. I couldn't believe how discreet they had been—we'd never noticed them.

Then, all of a sudden the Secret Service quickly and quietly cleared everyone from the floor except for the Burn Unit staff and family members. Dane and I looked at each other as if to say, *Well,* that *was pretty amazing.*

Finally I went in to see Brian. I was eager to see how he was doing.

His eyes were open for the first time.

My heart leapt when I looked into his beautiful green eyes. I said, "Hi, baby. How are you?"

He looked at me, then away, then back really quickly. His eyes followed me everywhere I went. While he couldn't say anything to me because of the tubes, he mouthed the words "I love you." Then he lifted his hugely bandaged arm and began to spell in the air with his fingers. Mostly he just kept spelling *pain* and *hurt.*

Then he began to barrage me with heavy questions: Did he lose any limbs? Did he still have an Army career? Did he still have a job? How was he going to support Matt and me?

I guess the drugs made him loopy because he put extra little curly things on his letters. Plus he's a bad speller! I couldn't figure out what he was spelling. I kept guessing wrong, and he'd get frustrated because I wasn't able to understand him. Or he would start to spell a word and get tired, and so I would try to figure it out for him. But at least he was communicating.

★　★　★

At around 11 A.M. President and Mrs. Bush arrived. They first visited two other Pentagon casualties on the third floor, then walked the flight of stairs to the Burn Unit ICU to visit the seven burn patients and their families. There was no media with them, no photo ops. Everything was hush-hush.

A nurse stepped in the room and said, "They're on their way." Colonel Rota and several members of the burn center staff came into the room with us—they wanted to see the President, too.

Mrs. Bush entered first. She had on a black suit with a lime green blouse, and she was absolutely gorgeous. I had never realized what a beautiful woman she is.

Before she came into the room, someone must have briefed the two of them, telling them who each person was and what his injuries were. So Mrs. Bush walked in and said, "Colonel Birdwell, it's nice to meet you. We're really proud of you, and you're an American hero."

I had to interpret for Brian. While he could mouth things, it was hard to read his lips since he had tubes in his mouth and nose. Spelling was a little easier than the lipreading—but not much since he was so bad at the fingering.

"Where are you from?" she asked him.

"He's from Fort Worth," I was able to answer.

She perked right up. "Really? I'm from Midland, Texas!"

And they put their hands up and did this little "Texas happy dance"—at least that's what I call it. It was as if two kindred spirits from Texas were reuniting. You know how when you meet someone you have something in common with and you want to get to know that person better? It was like that.

I think every Texan does this dance. *We're Texans, we bond, aaahhh.* I just laughed.

Then she asked if we had children, and I told her about Matt. She asked if we had pets, and I told her about our dog, Hayley.

Mrs. Bush and I talked for a few minutes, then she gave me a long, genuinely tender hug and asked how I was doing. I told her, "I'm doing okay."

She turned back to Brian and said, "Well, Colonel Birdwell, I brought someone to see you."

And . . . nothing.

She waited a moment, then turned her head toward the door. "I said I brought someone to see you, Colonel Birdwell." At that the President walked into the room. He looked haggard. His eyes were bloodshot, and you could tell his visit here was gut-wrenchingly difficult for him. He walked to the foot of Brian's bed, which was cranked up so Brian could "sit up" for the visit. Brian saw the President and his eyes were huge, so wide-eyed taking it all in.

The President said, "Colonel Birdwell" and saluted Brian. I couldn't believe what I was seeing. I was surprised that the President, as the commander-in-chief, subordinated himself to Brian, a junior officer. I thought, *He's showing respect for my husband.* My eyes filled with tears.

When the President began to drop his hand, he noticed that Brian was trying to return the salute.

Before President and Mrs. Bush arrived, the nurses had prepped Brian for the tank and surgery, so they had removed all his bandages. Only sterile towels were draped over him. As Brian tried to raise his arm, all we could see was bright red muscle—no skin. The skin had burned off, and the staff had debrided the rest.

The President stood still, with huge tears in his eyes, holding his salute while Brian tried desperately and agonizingly to return it. Brian struggled to lift his hand to a proper salute but was able to get only about three-quarters of the way up before he had to drop it because of the pain. President Bush continued to hold his salute until Brian's arm came back down.

Normally, the junior officer initiates a salute and then holds it until after the President drops his salute. In this case Brian struggled to lift his severely burned arm and hand to his forehead, while the President's arm stayed still. What an incredible moment. There stood the President of the United States—the most powerful man in the free world. And he was holding his salute to a junior-ranking officer—*my husband*—out of respect for him and what he was going through.

We were all crying. Finally President Bush dropped his salute and told Brian, "Colonel Birdwell, you are a great American, a hero, and we are going to get the guys who did this. This will not go unanswered." Brian seemed to take it all in with his huge eyes. Then the President turned to me, still with tears in his eyes, gave me a hug and a kiss, and asked how I was doing. I felt horrible because here was the President of the United States giving me a hug and a kiss—and I hadn't showered or washed my hair in three days! I had on no makeup. And my shirt had Brian's blood all over it because every time I would do something with Brian, such as help a nurse readjust his position, I would get his blood on me. *I'm making quite the impression*, I kept thinking. But President Bush didn't seem to notice.

Then Mrs. Bush explained pleasantly, "Colonel Birdwell is from Fort Worth." And it was the happy dance again! Even the President did the little Texas happy dance!

The President asked Brian, "Do you have children?"

"Yes, Sir," I told him. "Our son, Matthew. He's twelve."

He nodded solemnly.

"How about pets?"

"Hayley, our golden retriever. But Brian calls her the Big Stupid."

The President laughed at that. "Mrs. Birdwell, may we pray for your family?"

"Yes, please!" I said. "We'd really appreciate that."

Then he read my Vacation Bible School T-shirt, which said, "Every day's a holiday with Jesus in your heart"—the same T-shirt I had worn for the past two days.

"Is every day a holiday with Jesus in your heart?" he asked me.

"Yes," I said. "Some of them are not especially happy holidays, but every day is a holiday."

He chuckled, then asked, "Where is your church?"

I told him and he nodded. "I'm familiar with it."

Then one of the Secret Service agents stepped into the room. It was time for the President to move to the next family, the last burn victim. So they said good-bye and went into the next room.

It was an awesome visit, but very emotional for all of us. Brian was exhausted after that.

I thought about this historic visit. The leader of the free world had made time in his busy schedule to comfort us. He and the First Lady were so real, their compassion so genuine, and he was a man of God. This was a man who had seen the horror of burns, and I believe it further strengthened his resolve to respond to the terrorists' actions. I had looked into his eyes and could see he understood the gravity of what lay before this country—that by standing in Brian's presence, a potentially dying soldier, he would soon be sending other soldiers to their deaths by the decisions he would make in the upcoming days.

After the President and Mrs. Bush left, the nurse kicked us out of Brian's room so she could get him into surgery.

As Colonel Rota and I went out into the waiting room Army Specialist Pena from Walter Reed met us and handed me another packet for Brian's medical retirement.

I couldn't believe the audacity. Did they not understand my no?

Pena said, "Mrs. Birdwell, we need you to fill out this information."

I became livid. It was all I could do not to hurt her.

I had just listened to the President of the United States tell my husband he was a great American and a hero, and now the Army wanted to throw him out.

Rota saw me step toward the Walter Reed woman and jumped in between us.

"Mel, sit down," Rota said. "I'll handle this."

SPC Pena said, "Well, I was sent to give this to Mr. Birdwell."

"You mean, Lieutenant Colonel Birdwell," Dane corrected her.

She became flustered. "Yes," she said. Dane looked at her expectantly. "Yes, Sir," she said again.

He waited for me to sit down, then escorted Pena into the hall to get information on who he needed to talk to at WRAMC. He told Pena he'd take care of it, which he did. I'm not sure of all that happened other than he said he educated her—that things may have been done a certain way in the past, but all bets were off now. Then he assured me I wouldn't have to deal with the issue again.

After that incident, Dane forced me to go to the cafeteria. I went but didn't eat. I just wanted to get back up to Brian.

★ *Brian*

I was walking a fine line between life and eternity. I was in such excruciating pain, I begged God constantly to let me die. There was no reprieve.

The nurses kept me heavily drugged, both because of the burns and because of the treatment, so everything about my world was scrambled. I couldn't remember much of anything, except for a few images and parts of intensely emotional events.

I do remember hearing Mel's voice. It's so distinct—something of an Oklahoma drawl. And I loved hearing her talk to me, particularly when she read Scriptures. Her presence there kept me calm. I knew I wasn't alone.

I can't remember the first time I saw Mel, but I remember seeing her eyes. They were filled with an indescribable love and comfort, and they were filled with tears. Even in my drugged state I knew she would walk through this with me. I don't remember much else, since I was in and out of consciousness for most of the next couple of weeks.

I know my eyes were open when the President came, yet I don't remember the President's visit. I remember trying to salute. But I don't remember when. For some reason, I thought I was with the President in a laundromat. The medication was messing with my mind. But worse, it didn't help the pain. I still had intense, throbbing, searing pain all over my body.

When General Van Antwerp visited, I was alert enough to remember he was there. When I saw him, I asked about my coworkers Cheryle Sincock and Sandi Taylor.

General Van Antwerp paused and then shook his head mournfully. They were gone.

Gone. That one word exploded inside my head. I hit my head against the pillow and groaned. I didn't think I could feel worse pain than what I'd experienced up to this point. I was wrong. Knowing my coworkers were dead was worse than any of the burns or treatments I'd experienced.

Cheryle and Sandi were dead—and I was alive. A trip to the bathroom had saved my life.

Oh, God! I cried to myself. Immediately a concern filled me as I thought about their spiritual lives. I didn't know where Cheryle and Sandi had stood with God.

I wondered, *Did I do enough? Maybe I should have shared the gospel more. Maybe I should have told them more about Jesus.*

I vowed that if I survived, I would never live with another regret of having not shared my faith. I would never again give up an opportunity to tell someone about Jesus. I couldn't go back and witness to Cheryle and Sandi. But I could become more intentional about discussing my faith with others from this point forward.

★ *Mel*

After lunch Colonel Rota and I went back to 4H, where Major General Van Antwerp was waiting for us. General Van Antwerp was Brian's boss and a wonderful godly man and mentor to Brian. His frequent visits would prove to be a great comfort to both of us. Brian was out of surgery, and the general, a Christian, had already been in to see him and pray with him.

"Brian knew I was there, and we had a good visit," he told me.

We talked with the general for a while, then I went back to see Brian.

"I threw up on General Van Antwerp," Brian told me through his finger communication.

"What? You're kidding. He never mentioned that to me."

Later I asked the general about it. He chuckled and said, "Better me than the President."

Dr. Jeng came into Brian's room and told us he wanted to do a tracheotomy on Brian to ensure an open, clear airway. Because Brian was still at a high risk from his inhalation injury, Dr. Jeng was concerned that the passageway would swell too badly and Brian wouldn't be able to breathe. Dr. Jeng told us that because of the immense number of surgeries Brian was going to need, the physicians wanted to be able to use the trach to directly administer the anesthesia. He explained the best way to administer anesthesia is through the lungs. With so many upcoming surgeries, they couldn't keep intubating Brian each time since that would cause severe damage to Brian's throat. While I didn't like hearing that, I understood the importance of putting in the trach.

The Secretary of the Army, Thomas White, dropped by to visit Brian, which was a big deal considering White is one of the top men in the military.

Brian had another surgery that day. In each surgery they debrided him, scrubbed off the dead skin, and did skin grafts with synthetic pig or cadaver skin until he was infection-free and ready for his own skin to be grafted.

Each time was stressful for me; I knew every time he underwent anesthesia he could die. Plus the risk of infection grew greater with every day.

Later that afternoon my next-door neighbor Jolita phoned and asked, "What can I do? What do you need?" She was a godsend. I told her, "I need some clean clothes because I haven't showered in three days and I'm still wearing my clothes from Tuesday morning." So within a few hours she got a house key from my other neighbor, Sara, and brought me some clothes. I went over to my hotel room, took a long, hot shower, and changed outfits. I felt almost like a new person.

By this point the hospital had agreed to pay for one hotel room for all of the families to share, just to take turns taking naps and showers. Mostly we used it to bathe because what little we slept was in the ICU waiting room. After the first couple of nights, the hospital quickly realized none of us were leaving the ICU area. There was a conference room just down the hall from the ICU, so they graciously put roll-away beds in that conference room for us to get some sleep and still not have to leave the area. After that, the Red Cross offered to pay for each family to have a hotel room, so thankfully I had to pay for only one night.

As I thought about all that had happened in the last few days, I grieved. I worried about Brian and our future. But I also knew God was still in charge—even down to working out the details of our finances.

SEVEN

Unconsciousness Is Bliss

JOURNAL 9/17/01

He's exhausted and grouchy this morning. Didn't sleep last night and got no rest yesterday. He walked two laps today. I pretty much spent the day in his room, praying over every cell of his body, rubbing his feet, and just being there for him and for me. Read to him a lot and just enjoyed him being alive. Thank you, God, for sparing him.

★*Mel*

What is this? I wondered as I walked into Brian's room one morning and spotted a bright orange DNR sign on Brian's medical chart.

When Brian's nurse entered his room that morning, I asked, "Why is this here?"

She replied that someone from Walter Reed put it there that morning.

Then it hit me. DNR stands for Do Not Resuscitate.

I was angry. *Why are the people from Walter Reed doing this?* I thought. I ripped up the sign and threw it in the trash.

I went back into Brian's room and stood by the foot of his bed. My heart was slamming into my chest. I touched Brian's feet while he slept.

God, you can't let him die, I prayed. *You can't!* I began to pray over every cell in Brian's body. I started at his head and focused on each area, praying that God would supernaturally heal and strengthen him.

I hoped that was the only time I'd ever have to see a DNR sign on my husband's bed. But soon I discovered how fruitless that hope would be. The next several mornings I entered Brian's room, saw a new DNR sign on his chart, and ripped it off.

Finally, after several mornings of this, I'd had enough. I discussed it with Brian's nurse that day. And she assured me they didn't intend to honor that sign—that they'd do whatever it took to resuscitate Brian.

That was all I needed to hear. I never contacted WRMC to complain, because I knew the staff at the Burn Unit had things under control.

On Friday, September 14, John Collison, the officer who had escorted Brian to Georgetown, came to the hospital. I met him for the first time, hugged him, and thanked him for what he had done for Brian.

"I didn't know how badly hurt Brian was," John said, "until Dr. Williams at Georgetown told me, 'We'll know in six hours.'" John continued, " 'What do you mean you'll know in six hours?' I asked Dr. Williams. And he said, 'Because in six hours he'll either be dead or he'll still be alive.'" According to Dr. Michael Williams, Brian was probably five minutes from death from his inhalation injury. Had it taken five minutes more to get him to the hospital, he would not have survived.

It was an emotionally difficult visit for all of us because of what John had been through with Brian and how serious Brian still was. As soon as John saw Brian, John began to cry. He continually wiped his eyes and blew his nose into a red bandanna. He said, "Sir, it's good to see you. How are you doing?"

After the visit John mentioned to me that he had given Brian's ring to Colonel TW Williams, one of Brian's coworkers, because he thought Colonel Williams would be in to see Brian before John did. I hadn't really given Brian's ring any additional thought until John mentioned it. But once I heard about it, I became eager to get it. I called Colonel Williams to ask about it. He apologized for not making it to the hospital yet and assured me he would bring it as soon as possible.

Later that day a friend picked me up so I could go home and spend some time with Matt. The only reason I felt comfortable leaving Brian was because Brian's cousin Mike Ponder, a physician, offered to drive three hours from his home to spend the night with Brian.

At home I was unable to sleep or eat. I gathered some clothing, my makeup, which I hadn't worn since September 10 and desperately wanted to have, and my Bible, plus any information regarding our bills.

Earlier in the week a son of one of the patients offered to take family photos from all the victims' families to Kinko's to have them enlarged to poster size. That way we could hang them in the rooms. He thought that would bring some comfort to each victim. So while I was home, I grabbed several of our favorite photos: a picture of Matt and Hayley, our golden retriever, playing; a photo of Brian and Matt sitting together on a canon at a Civil War battlefield; and a family portrait we'd taken at Fort Leavenworth two years earlier. Brian was standing tall and trim in his Army uniform, his dark hair neatly combed. I was sitting in front of him smiling happily, as was our sweet red-haired son, Matt. After they were enlarged I would hang them on Brian's curtain.

I knew these photos would be especially important for Brian to see. Because of the large amounts of pain medication he was taking, he experienced hallucinations, such as thinking he was at the Metro in downtown DC or at a laundromat. If he could look at the photos, I thought he could tell himself, *Okay, I haven't left this room. No matter what my mind is telling me, this is where I still am.*

By eight o'clock Saturday morning, September 15, two friends from church, Dana Williams and Joanne Gerkins, dropped Matt and me off at the hospital.

The nurses had Brian up, forcing him to walk a lap in the ICU. They called the walk the "Bag and Drag"—because he was still on a ventilator, so they had to pack up all his "stuff"—IV pumps, oxygen, food bags, urine dispenser, rectal tube—and drag it along. He had quite the entourage of machines. They wanted him to walk every day to keep his muscles from atrophying.

It was exciting yet unbelievable to watch the staff get him up and start him walking. To think that on September 10 Brian had run almost five miles—and less than a week later it took two nurses and two physical therapists to help him walk even a few steps. While the walk was short, just around the nurses' desk in the middle of the ICU, it was incredibly painful. Brian was exhausted and took a long nap when he was finished.

Once more General Peake visited and asked where Matt was. I told him he hadn't yet seen Brian.

"Mel, you really need to get Matt in to see Brian."

"Thank you for your concern, Sir," I said firmly, "but my son just isn't ready yet to see his father." I knew Matt wasn't at a place where he could handle seeing how bad Brian looked. And even with everyone's good intentions, I knew no one knew my son as well as I did. I knew the time would come for Matt to see his father—it just wasn't now.

So Matt went back to stay with the Vances. It was so much easier for me at the hospital when I didn't have to worry about Matt and could focus totally on Brian. I felt guilty for feeling that way—especially because Matt was such a trooper. He kept telling me he understood I had to be there for Brian. Yet I could tell Matt really missed me and was trying to work through all of his emotions. Underneath it all, I don't think he really could understand everything that was going on. How could *any* kid? How could anyone?

Later General Eric K. Shinseki, Army Chief of Staff, and his wife, Patty, stopped by to visit. No sooner did the general clear the door than Brian was spelling *coin* in the air! The general pulled a special honorary Army coin from his pocket and gave it gladly.

After the general left, Brian mouthed to ask if I found his wallet and glasses.

"No, honey," I told him. "I've talked with the FBI, and they can't find your wallet."

"Did you cancel my government credit card?" he mouthed slowly while I struggled to understand.

"No."

"You need to do that, and you need to pick up my uniforms from the cleaners."

"Brian, I don't think you're going to need your uniforms for a while."

But he insisted. "You need to get my uniforms picked up from the cleaners!"

That was one of the best communications I had with Brian—even though it took a long time to figure out what he was mouthing! His questions brought back some semblance of normalcy; it showed me that underneath all the bandages and pain, my same wonderful husband was still there. I knew if he was tracking those things, then everything would be okay, because that's just what Brian would do. What a reassurance! It was these lighter moments I prayed for.

★ ★ ★

On Sunday, September 16, Dr. Jordan did a marathon five-and-a-half-hour surgery to autograft Brian's fingers. They used his abdomen as the donor site. Basically, this meant they used healthy skin from his abdomen to replace the charred skin on his fingers.

During the surgery I sat in the hallway, and when Katie, one of the surgical nurses, came out of the OR and said Brian looked beautiful in there, I was relieved beyond words. It was one more step in what was becoming a very long process. Little did I know how long the healing would take.

That first week I knew some of the details of what was happening to Brian. But I didn't know the *specifics* of what the hospital staff did. The old adage says ignorance is bliss. And I'm convinced that's true. I really think God shaded my eyes from a lot of the ugly details during that time so I didn't understand exactly what he was going through. I'm not sure I could have handled knowing the true extent of Brian's injuries and the excruciating hell he was living through.

Now that the ICU staff was allowing others besides me to see Brian, we had lots of visitors, including Brian's family—Wade, his brother; Liz, his sister-in-law; and Loretta, his mom. They arrived after the long drive from Texas.

Most of the visitors had a difficult time seeing Brian, especially the first time. Dennis Boykin, our close Army friend, came in, took one look at Brian, and in his most compassionate way, said, "Oh, you don't look too bad for a guy who got run over by a 757. Quit riding the profile. Get out of bed, and get back to work." And then Dennis went outside and wept.

Later that evening I went back into Brian's room to catch him tapping his foot, lip-synching to country singer Kenny Chesney's "She Thinks My Tractor's Sexy." I was so grateful that in the midst of such pain and tragedy we could still have moments of lighthearted laughter. While I shook my head at his antics and laughed, in my heart, I knew these moments would be few and far between. We had a long way to go.

The respiratory therapist started to adjust his ventilator to wean him from it. He was on it for four hours, then off for four hours. He began to cough excessively, which was good since he needed to get rid of the dead tissue from his lungs. The burned lung tissue had to be suctioned out by plunging a tube down Brian's throat to make him cough. This lung tissue, which looked like black cotton, came up through the tube. Coughing was terribly painful for him, obviously, because even *moving* was terribly painful. The nurse would usually push the tube down once. But Brian would have her plunge twice so he would cough more and bring up the tissue faster.

I thought, *That's overachieving there, buddy.* Once was bad enough, but to do it twice right away? That was inconceivable to me. It was just one of the ways in which Brian showed his toughness, his character, through this whole horrible ordeal.

The nurses would plunge, then he'd weakly lift his hand toward his throat and motion, as if to say, "Again."

The nurse, Michelle Howard, would say, "Are you sure?"

Brian would purposefully blink his eyes to say yes.

The nurse would look at me as if to say, *This is not right.* But the staff did it. I think they were pleased because they knew the dead tissue had to be removed—and the faster, the better.

I felt so helpless watching him suffer and not being able to take away any of his pain. Still the only part of his body I could touch was his feet. So I rubbed them constantly. Because he couldn't sleep, I stayed awake with him for days. Sometimes I slept fifteen or twenty minutes, but that was all. I became physically exhausted. Each time I'd try to sleep, my mind would race, and sleep just wouldn't come. I truly thought that if I stayed awake, nothing bad could happen to Brian. So to make the time pass, I talked to him incessantly. When I was too tired to talk, I read the Bible, especially the Psalms, to him for hours, hoping to find the comfort we both desperately needed.

★ *Brian*

I had been taken in and out of surgery more times than I could count.

The Sunday after the attack the doctors grafted all my fingers, which had third-degree burns. I still had my fingertips and fingerprints. My fingernails were still there, although they were badly burned. I lost all the webbing between my fingers on both hands.

Even though so much of my body needed grafting, the doctors were able to work only on my fingers because that was such an intricate job. Plus everything else was so badly burned I wasn't ready for grafting. My body was already fighting infections, and any time there's any infection they can't graft over it. My fingers weren't burned as badly, apparently, because Dr. Jordan was able to autograft them, meaning he was able to use my own skin on them.

Later that day General Keane, Army Vice Chief of Staff, visited with his entourage and briefed me on the damage to the Pentagon. I lay on my bed in shock as I listened to what had happened just five days earlier.

Al Qaeda terrorists hijacked American Airlines flight 77, flying from Washington's Dulles International Airport to Los Angeles. About a half hour after takeoff, the terrorists hostilely took over the cockpit and turned the plane back toward Washington DC—with their sights on hitting the Pentagon, the nation's symbolic fortress.

As the plane hurtled toward the building, it swept down so low, it clipped trees and utility poles on nearby Route 27 and a backup generator at the Pentagon. Flight 77 then smacked and bounced off the helipad before it smashed at a forty-five-degree angle into and through the twenty-four-inch-thick walls of the first and second floors of Rings E, D, and C, between corridors 4 and 5.

When the plane struck, there was apparently enough force for the tail to thrust itself through the aircraft and cockpit, then continue traveling through most of the Pentagon. Traveling at more than 350 miles an hour, and carrying sixty-four people, including children, the terrorists smashed the Boeing 757 into the west side of the building. Its point of impact: four windows from mine. They used the plane as a giant missile.

Ten thousand gallons of jet fuel spewed out of the wreckage, igniting a fire that reached more than 1,450 degrees. The fire was so hot that the firefighters could only move toward it for about five minutes at a time before their uniforms would melt. They would fight the fire and retreat, fight the fire and retreat. The fire blazed for more than twenty-six hours. Late Wednesday evening, September 12, they were finally able to extinguish it.

The Pentagon sprawls over twenty-nine acres and more than thirty thousand people are on its campus on any given day, many of them civilians. If there was one fortunate point about the place of impact it was that the terrorists hit the newly renovated section of the Pentagon. Not all the offices were occupied that morning because of the renovation, which was five days from being completed.

Part of the renovation included a reinforcement of the outer ring with floor-to-ceiling steel beams that ran through all five floors. Between the beams was a Kevlar-like mesh, similar to the material in bulletproof vests. Those reinforcements provided strength enough to keep the top floors from collapsing for about thirty-five minutes—time enough for many people to escape. That also stopped the concrete from becoming shrapnel in the blast.

The renovation included installing two-inch-thick, blast-resistant exterior windows that were covered with a Kevlar coating, making them blast-resistant. The windows above the crash site didn't shatter. And the new sprinkler system kept the fires from spreading through the entire building.

Yet even with the renovation, the damage was still tremendous. The crash damaged or destroyed two million square feet of office space. The extreme temperatures melted steel girders and turned sturdy concrete columns into piles of dust. It damaged more than four hundred support columns, some severely and some with microfractures. They would have to rebuild four hundred thousand square feet where the plane hit, an area nearly as large as seven football fields.

Demolition crews were working twenty-four-hour days, removing five thousand pounds at a time.

Not willing to kowtow to terrorists, the Pentagon would rebuild immediately. In fact, crews and Pentagon officials wanted the Pentagon rebuilt by September 11, 2002—one year to the day of the attack. And the one eerie fact: Ground for the Pentagon was broken originally on September 11, 1941.

I thought back to something General Keane said: The plane had come in at a forty-five-degree angle.

And I was fifteen to twenty yards from the point of impact, I thought. *If the airplane had come in straight, I'd be dead.*

The more General Keane talked, the more overwhelmed I became with the situation. Then I thought of Lieutenant Colonel Bill McKinnon, my friend who saved me in Corridor 4 at the Pentagon. I was afraid he didn't make it out, that he'd been found dead somewhere in the wreckage.

Intensely worried, I mouthed to Mel asking her about him. Mel didn't know why I was so concerned. I hadn't told her about my entire experience in the Pentagon since I still had to mouth everything, and telling the entire story would have been difficult with only mouth and hand gestures.

"Find out about Bill," I mouthed desperately to Mel.

Seeing my anxiety, General Keane's aide pulled out his phone and called someone to find out if Bill was among the missing.

Bill wasn't on the missing list, so the aide obtained Bill's home number and called him so Mel could speak to him.

★ Mel

Brian was extremely distressed about Bill McKinnon's status, and I couldn't understand why. I didn't know about Bill's role in Brian's recovery. But Brian was adamant about finding out how Bill was.

When the general's aide got Bill on the phone, I stepped out into the hall and spoke with Bill. That's when I learned Bill was one of the guys who helped get Brian out of the hallway and to the triage. I felt weak in the knees when I talked to him. I knew, without a doubt, that God had used Bill McKinnon to save my husband. I told him that when Brian was stronger, Brian would want to see him. Bill agreed to come when the time was right.

After I finished talking with Bill, I returned to Brian's room and told him Bill was fine and that he was looking forward to a visit.

I could see the huge relief in Brian's eyes.

EIGHT

What Happened?

JOURNAL 9/18/01

I have peace about this whole situation. I know God is sovereign and Brian is his. I still wig out and get scared, but God reminds me of his grace and sovereignty. Brian is only on loan to me. As I read the Psalms today I kept going back to the verse that reminds me the Lord is my rock and my fortress. I know I can crawl into his arms and rest!

★*Mel*

Every day in ICU seems to be a big day. But September 18 was especially hard. Antoinette Sherman died today. She was the worst of the burn victims. It was horrendous. Her mom, Eloise, Antoinette's boyfriend, Vincent, and I were in the waiting room when the nurse came out and said they were performing CPR on Antoinette and that it didn't look good. We began reading Psalms and praying and crying together. Eloise walked down to the ICU doors and stood staring in at Antoinette's room, watching the activity.

Less than half an hour later the nurse returned and told us that Antoinette didn't survive. It was so devastating for her precious family. Antoinette fought so hard but was too badly burned. She left behind a nine-year-old foster son, Jamal.

It was difficult to witness their pain, especially knowing that I, too, faced the same possibility of losing Brian. Yes, Brian was now conscious, but he was by no means out of the woods. Even with the lighter moments, he was still very much in danger of taking a turn for the worse.

It was more than a week before I spoke in depth with one of the doctors. They'd been almost constantly in surgery dealing with seven ICU burn patients. I just wanted Dr. Jordan to provide me some peace of mind and answers about Brian's prognosis. Dr. Jordan assured me that Brian was right on track with where he needed to be. However, because of the extent of his injuries, he would be in ICU for weeks.

I tried to spend as much time with Brian as the staff would allow. I brought in contemporary singer/worship leader Dennis Jernigan's CD *We Will Worship.* Brian was able to lip-synch praise songs. We both tried to stay focused on God and his sovereignty.

Several members of the Washington Redskins visited the hospital on September 18, so I made arrangements for Matt to come to the hospital to meet them. Matt still hadn't seen his father. Kristi, Brian's nurse, went into the lobby, where Matt was talking to the football players, and explained that she had Brian really cleaned up, that he looked good, it wasn't scary at all, and this would be a perfect time for Matt to see him. Matt was still uncomfortable and had to be convinced that seeing his dad was a good idea. Several of the players encouraged him and promised they'd be there for him, to help him be tough. Matt agreed. So seven days after the attack, our son made the courageous decision to visit his father.

★ *Brian*

I wanted to see my son so badly. I had asked about him since I became conscious, but I understood his anxiety and fears about seeing me. I could only imagine what I looked like.

Mel came into the room and told me about the Redskins wanting to visit. Then she said, "Matt's ready to see you today."

I was so excited, I could hardly wait. I decided I'd try my hardest not to show Matt my pain. And that was going to be a trick since I was still experiencing torture. But I wanted to be strong—just as I knew Matt wanted to be strong for me. Kristi placed blue towels all over my arms and head. Everything else was covered by the sheets. The only things Matt could see were portions of my face and my right foot sticking out from underneath the blanket.

While Mel helped Matt don a gown and gloves to keep my environment as germ-free as possible, the Redskins quarterback Jeff George and several other players also came into my room to visit. Normally that would have had me walking on cloud nine! But all I could think about was seeing Matt.

Finally Matt and Mel stepped into the room. I could feel my face light up when I saw him.

Matt stood there for a moment, taking me in. He was wearing a Redskins ball cap, and I could see his eyes beneath the cap go from fearful and cautious to anguish. He cried silently. I could tell he was trying to be brave. He took a deep breath and said in a quivering voice, "Hi, Dad." I lifted my arm as high as I could to wave and mouthed, "I love you, Bud."

There wasn't a dry eye in that room—even the Redskins players were teary-eyed.

It felt so good and so difficult at the same. What a great kid—and what a horrible thing he's had to go through. I think that was a big growing-up moment for Matt. It was certainly a growing moment for me. I'd have given anything for my son not to see his dad go through this horrific experience. I wish I could have sheltered him from that. But as with everything else in this circumstance, I was helpless to control anything.

I think what made the visit hardest is that, in our own ways, both Matt and I were wondering, *Is this the last time I'm going to see him?*

★*Mel*

I was so proud of Matt. I realized what a huge risk he was taking in seeing his dad. But I'm glad he did it in his time. We didn't stay long with Brian since I wasn't sure Matt could handle much on his first visit.

After we left, Matt asked about the thick, gooey, white substance on Brian's face. "Will he always look like that?" Matt wondered.

I explained, "That's Aquaphor. It's a medicine, a lot like Vaseline, that they put on his face to keep it moist." It was bizarre looking, but it wasn't permanent.

Matt appeared to be relieved by my answer. Now he had a picture of what Brian looked like, and I hoped that would help ease his mind on those sleepless, worrisome nights. I told him I loved him, then the Vances took him back to their house.

Brian was scheduled for another surgery—this time it was for an aggressive scrub to get rid of what Dr. Jeng called "the green stuff." Brian had developed a nasty, festering infection. The painful surprises never seemed to end.

★ *Brian*

The pain of the explosion was minor compared to the pain I now experienced—the scrubbings, the infection, the grafts, the swelling. Nothing took away the hurt completely. While some medications dulled the pain, my skinned, burned body refused to stop screaming out in anguish.

I began to pray for the times when I would go to surgery—at least then I would be knocked out and would experience some relief.

But mostly I lay in my hospital room, unable to move, unable to take away the pain. I spent a lot of time waiting. Waiting for the pain to go away, waiting for my body to heal. Waiting and thinking.

I thought back to the morning of September 11, the Tuesday that had changed my life forever. There was nothing to warn me about the abrupt change in my future.

The morning had seemed so normal.

I awoke at 4:45 A.M., my normal time, in order to catch the 5:35 A.M. bus to the Pentagon. I shaved, made my lunch, and opened the door to let our dog, Hayley, go outside. Then I prepared my satchel, in which I carried my T-shirt and socks so I could change into my Army uniform when I arrived at the office. I kept my shoes, belt, pants, and shirt at the Pentagon with all the other things I needed. The Pentagon has a dry cleaners on the premises, so I would take my uniform there to have it cleaned rather than drag it home.

I kissed Mel and Matt and was out the door at 5:30 to walk to the bus stop about a block from our home.

I rode the bus as I normally did, which put me at the Pentagon Metro station. As I walked through the station, I noticed the big digital clock that hung over the escalators read 6:25 A.M.

I stepped through the turnstiles at the street entrance and saw the defense protective service officers assigned to the Pentagon. I took out my Pentagon employee access badge and swiped it through the turnstiles.

Then I headed down the long halls toward my office area, 2E486—second floor, E-Ring, office 486—on the west side of the building.

I stepped into our department's conference room, changed clothes, and sat down at my desk. Our pastor often spoke of the importance of starting your day with God, so I had developed a habit of reading a devotional when I first arrived at work. That day I read part of a Charles Stanley devotional book, *On Holy Ground,* that I was working my way through. But there was nothing particularly memorable about it. No hidden message to prepare me for what was about to happen.

After I spent about fifteen minutes reading my book, I grabbed my ritual morning Coke and began my day as the military assistant to the Deputy Assistant Chief of Staff for Installation Management (ACSIM).

I scanned the day's headlines and some documents. Then I checked my boss's and my e-mail, and checked over my boss's calendar to make sure everything was set for the day.

I greeted my coworkers as they arrived and chatted for a bit about normal things—the day, what we had done the night before, the impressive heat wave our area was experiencing for a late summer day.

Fortunately, not all my coworkers were in the office that day. Major General Robert L. Van Antwerp and my boss, Jan Menig—a member of the Senior Executive Service (SES), the civilian equivalent to a general—had been in the office earlier but left around 7:45 for a garrison commanders conference across the street at the Doubletree Hotel. Once a year all the installation—military base—commanders throughout the Army get together to discuss the latest policies and programming.

The only other coworkers in were Colonel TW Williams, my counterpart, who was General Van Antwerp's military aide, Cheryle Sincock, General Van Antwerp's secretary, and Sandi Taylor, Staff Actions Control Officer for ACSIM.

Another coworker, Clara Toland, Ms. Menig's secretary, usually arrived around ten o'clock. However, that day she was on leave because she was caring for her ill aunt.

Colonel Williams was in the office for a period of time, then stepped out to run errands.

At around nine o'clock, Sandi's phone rang; it was her daughter, Sam, who worked in New York City. Sam told her mom to turn on the television—the World Trade Center had been hit.

Sandi got up quickly from her desk and said, "Sam just called and said a plane hit the World Trade Center." Cheryle and I also got up from our desks and followed Sandi into Ms. Menig's office, where the television was.

Sandi turned on the TV, and the three of us stood in Ms. Menig's office and watched all the smoke pouring from the World Trade Center in New York City.

Immediately, Cheryle, Sandi, and I knew something wasn't right. The newscasters were speculating that it might have been a Cessna plane that hit the building.

"That was no Cessna," I said. It was a clear blue sky with no weather issues. It didn't look like an accident.

We discussed the traffic patterns for LaGuardia and Kennedy. We knew no pilot would run a plane into a building—even if the plane experienced a catastrophic mechanical failure. A pilot would put it in the water to try to hurt as few people as possible. We knew this couldn't be a plane simply having a problem with its takeoff because at that altitude, the traffic patterns of Kennedy and LaGuardia are all on the east side, not the west side of New York, the side where the World Trade Center sat.

"There's no way that's an accident," I murmured. We kept discussing how it didn't look like weather was a problem. It wasn't instrument failure. This was either a catastrophic failure at a critical point in a critical path—something that would be so improbable it would be truly incredible—or it was a deliberate crash.

By this point, I'm sure there were people inside the Pentagon who were starting to take action, but our division wasn't one of them. My department was Installation Management. We handled issues that were military-base-infrastructure related, such as military-base construction, environmental issues, things like that. We were just spectators like everybody else. So when the phone would ring, it was mostly from other spectators in the Pentagon saying, "Have you seen this?" For the most part, it was quiet because everybody else was watching the tragedy on TV.

At about 9:20 we watched the second plane enter the camera shot really quick on the right side and go behind the first tower. The next thing we saw was a huge explosion. That confirmed it for us. Now we knew this was no accident; this was a terrorist act.

We were shocked. It was difficult to watch, knowing that people were in those planes and those buildings and that we were watching their murders. I didn't want to imagine the horrors they were experiencing. I began to realize the logistical nightmare the emergency personnel were experiencing. Two of the world's largest buildings were on fire, and they were at elevations far higher than fire equipment would reach. Worse, the buildings were located in a very constricted area with lots of people, jammed traffic, and roads not wide enough to accommodate the traffic and the emergency vehicles.

I felt helpless and weak. I returned to my desk, which was just outside Ms. Menig's office, to pray. That was the only thing I could do. *Lord, be with the fire and police folks in New York at those buildings,* I began.

For some reason, I never thought to call Mel. Usually Mel calls me about major news events. But she never phoned—and I never thought to contact her. Thinking about it now, I realized God must have blocked that thought from my mind. I wasn't supposed to talk to Mel.

Sandi's phone rang again. Sandi ran out around all the modulars in the open office area to catch her phone. It was her daughter, Sam.

This time Sam called to tell Sandi to get out of the building. Sam was concerned that the Pentagon would be a terrorist target. Sam told Sandi that she had a bad feeling about the Pentagon—and pleaded with Sandi to please evacuate as soon as possible.

Sandi told us what Sam had told her, but we disregarded it.

"No," I said. "Not the Pentagon."

There was never a fear—or even a serious thought—that we would be next.

"Those terrorists would have to be real idiots to go after the defense headquarters of the United States of America," I said as I sipped my morning Coke. "If they did that, they'd have the entire United States military after them."

It must have been about fifteen minutes after that second plane hit that I felt the effects of the Coke. So I stood up and told Sandi and

Cheryle, "I'll be back in a moment." Sandi was in the doorway to Ms. Menig's office still watching the television. Cheryle had stepped back into the main office area to start working again. I stepped out of the office, turned to the right, and walked down the hall toward Corridor 4, then took a left toward the men's room. It was about fifteen to twenty yards away from our department, about the length of two cars.

That would be the last time I spoke with Cheryle and Sandi.

★ ★ ★

I lay in the hospital bed and thought about Craig Sincock, Cheryle's husband, and the pain he must be enduring.

Then I thought about Sam, Sandi's daughter. I can't imagine what she felt when she discovered that the Pentagon, in fact, had been hit— and her mom didn't survive. To have a sense of impending doom, to call her mother and tell her, "Get out of the building!" Then to have her worst fears realized. My heart ached for her.

Yet there was no other warning of the danger. There was no sound of the roar of jet engines. Nothing.

Had I spoken with Mel and left twenty seconds later, I would have been in the path of the plane as I headed toward the restroom. Had I left for the restroom twenty seconds sooner, I would have been directly in the path of the plane upon my return from the restroom.

I lay on my bed and grieved the loss of my two close, dear coworkers.

I thought back to September 7, the Friday before the attack on the Pentagon, when our department had had a late-summer picnic. I remembered Sandi Taylor laughing and smiling during the day. She had worn a beautiful wide-brimmed hat and a multicolored dress, a departure from the muted tones she wore for work. I had even made a comment about how bright and fun she looked. Now that memory was bittersweet.

As difficult and as painful as everything had been for me physically up to this point, that pain was nothing compared to the finality of losing my coworkers. The emotional ache was much deeper. It reached way down into my soul and ripped a part of me that I knew would never quite be whole again.

★ *Mel*

Colonel TW Williams, the other military aide in Brian's department, visited Brian. Brian had been concerned about Colonel Williams. Even though Williams had been running errands the morning of September 11, Brian didn't know if he had returned to their office while Brian went to the restroom, right before the attack. Brian was relieved when he learned Colonel Williams had never reentered that section of the building.

Before we entered Brian's room, TW pulled me aside and handed me something. I looked down at his hand. It was Brian's wedding ring. As soon as TW handed it to me, I put it on and wore it next to my wedding ring. I decided I would return it to Brian after he was discharged from the hospital.

I wasn't aware of the exchange Brian and John Collison had with the ring or the significance of the way it was removed because John had never mentioned it. His visit had been too emotional. But I knew that John had received Brian's ring at some point; I just wasn't sure when.

On September 20 Brian slept most of the day. He had surgery at 2 P.M. Dr. Jeng told me afterward he did some very aggressive scrubbing and told the staff to "frost him like a cake." In other words, Dr. Jeng ordered them to pile on the Silvadene, an antimicrobial ointment that they lathered over his burns before they dressed him with bandages.

Brian had a raging infection and fever. He also developed a heart arrhythmia and a racing heart rate. The staff began to monitor him closely and considered increasing the medication, Lopresser, to slow down his heart rate. They were concerned about getting his rate back under control. The problem was that because burns can shut down your internal organs, they can also shut down your heart. So from that point forward every day they did an EKG on him. The arrhythmia never presented itself again, but the rapid heart rate did. I was so scared—it felt as if everything was happening at once. And nothing was under our control.

Later that afternoon I received a call from Dave Davis, who worked for the office of Kay Bailey Hutchinson (U.S. senator from Texas), asking if I'd like to attend the President's address to the Joint Session of Congress that evening. I talked to Brian about it, and he encouraged me to go. So Colonel Dane Rota, my right-hand man, drove me to Hecht's, a local clothing store, to buy an appropriate suit and shoes to wear. I've never shopped so quickly in my life. I walked into the store and fifteen minutes later came out with an outfit in tow! I rushed to the hotel to shower and get ready. But while I was in the shower, I started to hyperventilate and had a massive panic attack. I couldn't breathe and became dizzy. I thought I was having a heart attack. I became overwhelmed with fears that there would be an attack on the Capitol building that night. *What would happen to Matt?* I worried. I stood in the shower and cried and prayed frantically. I just couldn't get any peace about going.

I quickly got out of the shower and called Dave back, explaining the situation as calmly as I could. He was very kind. I think he really did understand my fears. So I put on my jeans and T-shirt again and walked back to Brian's room. We watched the speech together on TV.

In Psalm 27:7-8, King David writes,

Hear, O Lord, when I cry with my voice,
and be gracious to me and answer me.
When You said, "Seek My face," my heart
said to You, "Your face, O Lord, I shall seek.

As I sat in Brian's room that night and watched the President, I thought about those verses and claimed them as my own. They were God's personal promise to us—that he would carry Brian and me through this. I needed to keep my focus on God, and he would handle all the other things.

After the President's speech, I opened my Bible and began to read Philippians 4:13 to Brian: "I can do all things through Him who strengthens me." It was another verse I would cling to in the days to come.

NINE
Aftereffects

JOURNAL 9/19/01
The staff is upping Brian's antibiotics and amnesia medication to help him forget his pain. He was totally out of it. He couldn't stay awake for anything. That's a good thing. He needs the rest.

★*Mel*

Every day it felt like I was riding a roller coaster. Brian still wasn't able to speak because of the trach. But he mouthed lots of words. He blew me kisses and told me I was his queen. Those were the high times.

The low times were extremely low. The doctors were having trouble containing his staph infection. Burns are highly susceptible to infections, which can take root in the dead tissue and eat away at the body. There are two kinds of staph infection—regular staph and hospital staph. Hospital staph is the worst kind because it perpetuates itself and becomes extremely resistant to antibiotics.

Brian had hospital staph. They kept trying to treat his infection with massive doses of antibiotics, but nothing would kill it.

Every time I walked into his room, the smell of the infection would just about knock me over. It was a distinctive and sickening odor.

The infection covered all of the burned areas on his body with green pus. It was eating away at his face and ears. It was even in his eyes.

Plus Brian's arms were still festering. Dr. Jeng had to perform another extreme surgery in which they put him under anesthesia and scrubbed him. Dr. Jeng told me they were going to use a bleachlike solution to kill the infection; it was essentially the equivalent of scrubbing Clorox on his arms.

They also used a diluted bleach-type substance to soak his bandages in before they dressed his wounds, hoping that would cure the infection. That was so incredibly painful for him that they had to double his pain medication. I prayed fervently that God would ease his pain.

When after a week and a half that treatment still didn't kill it, Dr. Jeng entered Brian's ICU room to speak with me.

"Okay, here's the plan," he began—but to me he sounded a little too excited. "We're doing maggots."

I stared at him blankly for a moment, letting his words sink in.

"I've already spoken to Brian, and he agreed," he continued. "But he wanted me to tell you because he didn't think he could really explain."

"We're doing maggots—*on purpose?*"

"Yep. The nurses prefer to call them sterile larvae, since they feel the word *maggots* is too harsh. But let's not sugarcoat it; they're maggots."

I swallowed hard. "Why?"

"The maggots eat the dead tissue and leave the good, healthy stuff. They do a better job of removing the bad stuff than we can. Brian's infection is at the point where we have to take extreme measures."

Then as if to comfort me, he said, "We can have them shipped overnight to arrive by 10 A.M. tomorrow morning. They will be on him for three days. We place them in clear, long plastic bags, then put the bags over Brian's arms with this brown goo."

"Will that take care of the infection?" I asked.

"It should," he responded.

By that point I thought, *Okay. Whatever it takes to get Brian well, let's do it. If you want me to go pick the maggots off a dead animal on the side of the road, I'll do that. I'll get whatever he needs to have.*

When the maggots, or sterile larvae, arrived, I thought I would gag. Combined with the stench from the infection and the green pus, only the sight of these ugly little creatures could have been worse. The nurses put Brian's arms in a bag of brownish, maggot-filled juice. And as the maggots ate, you could see chunks of pus-looking gunk with bits and pieces of muscle tissue floating in the bag. It was ghastly.

For three days Brian and I watched the maggots eat to their fill and grow. Brian could even feel them wiggle around on his arm. Fortunately they didn't cause him pain—and they worked. Those little divinely created creatures worked wonders. Somehow God created those maggots to know exactly what tissue is dead and what's not—right down to the cell level. For Dr. Jordan or Dr. Jeng not to use them and to debride Brian to get rid of the infection using a surgical instrument, would have been the equivalent of gutting him like a fish. For every piece of dead tissue they took out, they would take ten times as much good tissue. The maggots did a better, more precise job than what a surgeon could do with his scalpel.

★ Brian

At night the nurse closed the curtain to my room, and I was supposed to sleep. But I could see this yellow light through the curtain. I lay there for hours every night with the bed propped up, since they wouldn't allow me to lie flat because of air constrictions. I would stare at that light, not interacting with anybody, just counting the seconds and minutes.

I felt like a prisoner. My only surroundings were my room, the tank, and the nurses' station that I shuffled laps around. For twenty-six days, the time I spent in the ICU was all I knew.

On September 10, I jogged four and a half miles—from my Pentagon office, over a Potomac River footbridge, to the Teddy Roosevelt island, and back. I weighed 168 pounds. I was in the best physical condition of my life, and I felt great.

Two days later even standing up was a challenge. The first time the nurses asked me to walk, two steps exhausted me.

I was so swollen from the fluid building around the burns that I weighed more than 200 pounds.

Each day in the ICU was essentially the same. It was a day-by-day, hour-by-hour observation. I experienced daily debriding, tank sessions, redressing of my wounds, and physical therapy.

Every four hours the nurse administered my pain medication—which usually wore off after two to three hours. It was torturous to have to wait for my next dosage. They had to give me serious dosages of pain killers for everything—because everything they did caused tremendous pain above and beyond the initial pain from the burns.

I was on several different medications. For the pain they gave me Dilaudid, a morphine derivative. I was on Adavan (an antianxiety medication), Diprivan (a sedative), and Versed (an amnesia drug), to help me forget. Benadryl was to help me sleep and to stop the itching once I started to heal. Everything was administered through my IV. But the quantities of Dilaudid they had to administer were unbelievably high since it only dulled the pain but never completely relieved it.

In the mornings after the nurses administered the medication, it was time to remove my bandages. The bandages had to stay moist continually so they wouldn't stick to my skinless body.

The nurses cut the bandages and unwrapped me. Many times even though the dressings were wet, the pieces of gauze stuck and would have to be pulled off the muscle or tissue, revealing an oozing, pus-filled wound.

Once that work was completed, I was placed on a gurney totally naked except for a light blanket. The nurses pushed my gurney around the nurses' central station and into a room with a giant whirlpool—the tank.

They placed me on a board made of hard rubber, strapped me to it so I wouldn't fall off, then dipped me in the tank. The tank was filled with a warm water-chlorine-iodine mixture. Once I was submerged, they either cut away any nonviable tissue, or they scrubbed it off. They took towels and washed every burned area to clean it and to remove the dead tissue. It was like dousing an open wound with alcohol—and it was my entire body. After they finished the scrubbing, they lifted the board and rinsed me.

I couldn't move. I could only watch them scrub my arms and legs. I was a captive, and all I could do was pray for them to hurry and get me to surgery as quickly as possible. I kept thinking, *Get it over with. Get it over with. Hurry.* From the tank, they would often take me directly into surgery. That was the best part because the anesthesiologist would conk me out—the only time I was pain-free.

Because of the amnesia medication, I don't remember much. The amnesia drugs didn't relieve the agony, they just helped me not to remember it. Sometimes they didn't up the dosage enough—and I remembered everything. I remember very clearly at least five times in that dreadful tank. It hurt getting out of bed. It hurt getting on the gurney. It hurt being rolled to the room and then placed inside the water. Then came the intense sting, like little needles pricking every inch of my body.

Once I was wet, the nurses began to debride me. It felt as if they were using steel wool washcloths—on top of the stinging. They were wiping a washrag over open wounds where, in some cases, it was directly on straight muscle. It was absolutely agonizing.

One day it was so bad I didn't think I was going to survive. I begged them to give me more pain medication, but they wouldn't because I was going into surgery right after the tank session, and they were afraid the amount of medication would compromise the anesthesia. Finally Dr. Jeng came in and told me they couldn't give me any more pain medication. It was Dr. Jeng's way of saying, "Suck it up." It just broke my heart. I felt as if I was drowning, barely holding to the life preserver, and they ripped it from me.

Those memories terrified me. The moment when I would see the nurses roll in the gurney, I would tremble with the knowledge of what was coming next. Many days I would beg, "Just let me lie here and die. Please!"

I remember distinctly another day when I was really worried about a tank session coming up. The day before, my night nurse, Michelle Howard, had given me some sort of amnesia medication just as they were bringing in the gurney to take me to the tank. They placed the gurney beside my bed, and I knew what was coming. It was like telling a convicted criminal, "Sit in the chair. We're going to juice you." But I didn't remember much after that. The next thing I knew, I woke up back in bed. It was as if they were saying, "Oh yeah, your tank session is done."

But the next day I had a different nurse because I was going in the tank at a different time. She didn't give me the same drug Michelle had given me. I told her adamantly, "You've got to give me that same drug again."

She answered, "No, we can't do that."

I was in hell. I remember vividly everything about that tank session. It wasn't only the pain of what they were doing to me physically; it was the mental torture and anguish of knowing they could do better than what they were doing. I thought, *I know you can give me this drug. I'm not having surgery after this. You did it to me just two days ago. Now why won't you give it to me again?*

The amount of time I spent daily in the tank was about fifteen minutes. But to get to and from the tank was an hour.

The nurses changed my bandages twice daily. I visited the tank once a day unless I'd had surgery. In which case I didn't go to the tank for five days afterward.

On the days I didn't have surgery, after the tank session, they returned me to my room and rebandaged me. First, they placed Silvadene on my body to act as a cooling and soothing agent—although not much for me was cool and soothing. They put the Silvadene, a white topical ointment, on a large rectangular bandage, then wrapped it around the burn area. They started with my arms and curled it like gauze. Then they wrapped the bandages on my fingers. Finally they turned me over and put them on my back. After they placed all the bandages, they wrapped this jacket-type article on and safety-pinned it together to keep the dressings in place.

After a skin graft surgery, they would apply a yellow petroleum-like ointment wrapping called Xeriform. It contains a special substance that keeps the graft lubricated so it doesn't stick to its covering.

They changed the Silvadene twice a day. The Xeriform was removed after three days. They tried to do the bandage changes around ten in the morning and then again at ten at night.

The dressing changes and the debriding in the tank took almost three hours daily.

Then there were the surgeries. I was in surgery almost every day it seemed. I didn't mind that; actually, I looked forward to those times since that was the only time I was relieved of pain. Yet even in my sleep I felt the slicing and throbbing.

The surgeries were for debridements, excisions, and to graft new skin onto my body.

The heat that's generated from a burn literally cooks the water out of the skin. The skin goes from being a flexible living thing to something more like a tanned leather belt.

There are three layers of skin: the epidermis, the dermis, and the hypodermis. With a first-degree burn, the top layer, the epidermis, has been burned away. A second-degree burn means the dermis and the epidermis have been burned away. With first- and second-degree burns the third layer of skin is still there, as well as the hair follicles, oil glands, sweat glands, and temperature sensors. Everything is still resident inside your third layer of skin, the deepest layer—including the skin pigment. With a third-degree burn, every layer of skin is gone. It's called a full thickness burn, meaning that skin is completely gone. And what's directly exposed is muscle.

A third-degree burn cannot regenerate skin. So the third-degree burn must be closed by skin grafts. They prefer to take skin from other parts of your body that hasn't been burned. Otherwise, they have to grow tissue in a lab, import it from other burn centers, or use cadavers or pig skin.

They used all of the above on me. My arms and forehead had to have pig and cadaver skin as temporary grafts until my infections were under control enough to use my own skin. Fortunately, since my stomach and upper thighs escaped unscathed, they were able to use that skin as a donor site.

I was burned over 60 percent of my body, with more than 40 percent third-degree burns. That's a lot of skin grafts.

My arms were complete third-degree burn losses. Everything was gone. If a burn is circular, in which a small portion of it is third-degree, the second-degree and first-degree burn area around it could eventually grow laterally and cover that area. But because I had such a large area that was third-degree burns, my arms had to be completely grafted.

My stomach served as the donor site for my fingers, elbows, and face. For my arms, Dr. Jeng used my upper thighs.

After the cadaver or pig skin has been grafted, the body will eventually reject it, or it will rot off. So skin grafting isn't a one-shot deal. As the skin starts to rot, the staff debride it, clean up the area, and put more on. It's like working with adhesive bandages: Once you have a Band-Aid that's soiled, you take that Band-Aid off and put on a new one. They don't graft on cadaver skin and think it will last for the next six weeks while you wait for your own skin to be ready. You have to keep changing it.

For autografts, using a burn survivor's donor sites, doctors shave the hair on the donor site, then slice off the top two layers of skin. They use a dermotone, an instrument that has a very sharp, flat blade that moves back and forth at about 270 strokes per second. I compare it to taking a cheese slicer to a block of Velveeta. Essentially where they remove that donor skin, they create the equivalent of a second-degree burn, because they leave only the lowest level of skin.

Donor sites can be used more than once because the skin grows back faster. The reason they'll go to a donor site a second time is because after a few weeks the body is still healing that area, so the skin is rich in nutrients.

The skin grafts were exceedingly torturous. But the area that hurt the most after a grafting surgery was the donor site. While my arms would hurt, it wasn't nearly as much or intensely as the donor site. Once the doctors shaved off the skin, to protect that donor site, they would cover it with a substance called glucan, which is glued and then stapled on. It would stay in place for several days, then the staples were taken out on the third day. The glucan would gradually peel off after that. As with everything else, this hurt. If the staple went in straight it would come out straight. If it went in crooked, it would hurt coming out. But if the glucan started to peel off before it should, a nurse could accidentally tug on it. More pain.

After they've sliced off the skin, they put it in a perforator to allow a one-square inch area of skin to cover two square inches. That way they don't have to take as much skin to cover you. This causes a checkering look to the healed grafted area.

After they slice off the skin, they place that graft in a bowl of sterile saline to keep it moist until it's time to place it on the wound. When they place it, they staple it in to ensure it stays put.

Part of the problem with having skin grow around and over the burned skin, though, is that when the skin around it grows back, it grows into what is called skin buds; it's very granular and grows lumpy. And that's bad. They don't want granulation because it causes raised and bumpy scaring underneath. So they go in before they graft and shave that off so it's smooth and level before they put a graft on.

★*Mel*

I was with Brian every moment I could be. The only times they insisted I leave was during his tank sessions, dressing changes, and physical therapy—which was about six hours each day. The first week and a half Brian was in ICU, they didn't enforce visiting hours. I could come and go any time day or night. So I stayed with him a majority of the time, sitting by his bed. When he was awake, I would talk or read the Bible to him. And when he was asleep or "out of it," I would read or watch TV or write in my journal. I would bring mail in with me and read that. Anything to make the time pass.

But some days that ICU and Brian's small room felt oppressively claustrophobic. I had to get out of there. I would wait for him to fall asleep so I could get a reprieve from the suffocating closeness of sickness and death and pain. I would pray for him to sleep so I could rush out in the hallway just to breathe.

★ Brian

Because I had an inhalation injury, I had to have chest X-rays every day to check the status of the injury. They would bring in a portable X-ray machine, prop me up until I could hardly breathe, and tell me to take a deep breath and hold it.

There were also the daily physical therapy sessions to keep contractures from forming. Otherwise I would be frozen in whatever position the scars determined. But that therapy was painful, too.

Actually, there wasn't anything that didn't cause tremendous amounts of pain. If I don't recall something, it was because I was so often out of my mind with the pain. Most days there wasn't much that didn't hurt, with the exception of Mel rubbing my feet. Even with the amount of medication I was on, I was still either physically hurting or in a drug-induced hallucination, a brain scramble.

★ Mel

I didn't sleep except maybe fifteen minutes here and there for the first two weeks. And every time I tried to eat something I became physically ill. This was unusual for me, because normally when I feel stressed, I grab as much chocolate or comfort foods as I can. But not now. How could I sleep? or eat? Everything was too stressful. Even drinking anything was a stretch for me.

While I believed with all my heart Brian would survive, the staff was very clear about the fact that Brian's burns put him in a pretty significant risk group for dying.

They kept Brian heavily sedated while in ICU. Many times it didn't matter what they gave him—it didn't help.

Before every surgery, every bath, every dressing change, Brian and I prayed together and I read to him Joshua 1:9: "Have I not commanded you? Be strong and courageous! Do not tremble or be dismayed, for the Lord your God is with you wherever you go." We relied completely on God's presence to get us through those agonizing moments.

I also became Brian's most loyal advocate. When the day nurse gave the night nurse a report and then the night nurse had to come into Brian's room, I gave him or her a report at Brian's direction. I would list off everything that he wanted to have done, and if I forgot something, he would remind me. They indulged us.

Everything became a waiting game. After so many operations, I began to know how long a surgery would take. I would get to the end of that waiting period and if Brian wasn't out yet, I'd feel big knots in my stomach.

One day while Brian was in surgery, Matt and I sat and worked on his math outside the Burn Unit's operating room, which had an entrance directly from the hallway. All of a sudden I heard the staple gun going off. I panicked, knowing Dr. Jeng was stapling skin to Brian's burn areas. I said, "Okay, Son, we have to go do math somewhere else." Matt didn't know what had happened. But I did. And I didn't want to hear what was going on in there. It became too difficult not to imagine some horrible thing they were doing to my husband. I never again sat that close to the OR while Brian was in there.

TEN

Previous Pain

JOURNAL 9/23/01
God, I know you've been preparing me for this for a while; I just didn't expect my trials would come through Brian. Yet I thank you for the ways you've prepared me for this, for the tremendous privilege of being Brian's wife, and for allowing me to love him and help care for him. Thank you, Lord, for sparing his precious life and restoring us as a family.

★*Brian*

While we had never experienced anything as devastating as September 11, Mel and I were no strangers to pain and tragedy. But what we faced now seemed insurmountable. If it wasn't for our belief in God, we would have struggled even more intensely. What helped us work through this current situation was that we had proved our faith before, in other life circumstances.

I'm a product of a broken home. Originally from Fort Worth, Texas, I was nine months old when my parents divorced. My mother was awarded custody of my older brother, Wade, and me. When I was about four years old, Mom met and married Patrick Reves, a very godly man. Soon after, we moved to Austin then to California in 1966, where we remained for seven years until we moved back to Texas. Mom had us for the school year and Dad had us for four weeks in the summer and for a week every other Christmas.

In 1971 we were living in Stockton, California. I was ten when we attended a James Robison crusade in the Stockton Civic Center. They gave an altar call, and both Wade and I felt the Lord's tug on our hearts. We made our decision to give our lives to Christ. Pat, my stepfather, is the primary reason I grew closer to Jesus. He modeled a real genuineness and a love for God.

But even living in a Christian home and starting a personal relationship with Jesus didn't guarantee a perfect life.

My parents' divorce had caused a significant personal struggle for me—even though I was so young and had no memory of my father living in our home. I felt as if I had to change identities and allegiances whenever my parents traded custody for the summer and every other Christmas. Texas and California were two separate worlds in which I lived two different lives with almost two different personalities.

I determined early on that I would never discuss one parent with the other. The tension was always there but was especially thick during the "exchange" moments. Dad would drive to California, pick us up, throw our bags in the back, and drive back to Texas, where Wade and I would spend the summer with him and our cousins and relatives. Then when it was time to go back to California, during the two days of nothing but driving, my mind would race with the dreaded thoughts of the upcoming exchange and being in the presence of both parents. When we'd pull up to the house, I would ring the doorbell to let Mom know I was home. Pat, my stepfather, would come out to greet us. I never handled the situation well; Wade was always a better diplomat between Mom and Dad and Pat. While I chose to act as if nothing was happening, the reality was that it really hurt. In fact, it hurt so much that I didn't want to have anything to do with anybody.

I never discussed what I did with the other parent without feeling as if one parent was checking on the other. When Mom would ask, "What did you do this summer?" I was suspicious of her motives—and the same for my father. I felt as if the questions were asked to imply, *Whom would you choose? Whom do you love more?*

To this day I still carry those emotional scars. It's the unfortunate side of divorce. And it brought me tremendous pain.

★ *Mel*

I grew up in an unstable home. It was a rigid existence, one with few happy memories.

My one safe haven was my grandma's house. Every weekend Mom would pack my older sister, Connie, my younger brother, Tony, and me into the car. We would drive to my grandma's, my memmie's.

I grew up going to church with Memmie. She used to take me to church camp with her every summer and Sunday school every week. She was a godly woman and a huge positive influence, which I needed desperately.

When I was eight, Tony, who was almost seven, was playing T-ball. We went to his game to cheer him on. He was standing at third base when a player hit the ball toward him. Everyone gasped when the ball struck him hard in the chest.

Tony took a step and threw the ball. Then he collapsed. Immediately a group of people ran onto the field. I was so scared I ran to Mom's car and hid in the backseat. I rocked back and forth and prayed and pleaded for Tony to be okay. I just kept crying and praying.

Tony was rushed to the hospital. The doctors said the ball had struck him in the chest between heartbeats. He was hospitalized for twenty-one days.

I didn't see Mom or Dad the entire time Tony was in the hospital. I was shuffled from family to friends to whomever could take care of me while they were at the hospital with him.

One day I was at Memmie's house, playing her piano in the living room. My aunt arrived, and she and Memmie went into the kitchen and spoke in hushed tones. I knew they were talking about Tony so I went in. They both stopped their conversation and looked at me. When I didn't move, Memmie said, "Honey, your brother just died."

Her words felt as if I'd been hit by that ball too. My chest was so tight it hurt. But I didn't cry. I walked out of the room alone.

I knew what *dead* meant. I knew I would never see my little brother again. And I didn't know what to do. Tony and I had been really close. We'd cried together and comforted each other. But mostly I knew I would miss our times together before bed. Tony and I shared a room, and every night we'd dress up our dog in doll clothes. She'd lie indulgently in bed with us, wearing those ridiculous clothes, until we fell asleep. And then she'd escape, and Mom would take the doll clothes off her.

I couldn't believe my brother was dead. But I never cried until the funeral. Then I crawled up in my uncle Gary's lap and sobbed. Until that moment I had carried that heavy weight alone.

After Tony died, I continued to attend church with Memmie. And when I was thirteen, I accepted Jesus into my life at Falls Creek Church Camp. Charles Stanley was the guest speaker that week.

While I know I accepted Jesus at that camp, I didn't understand everything about that commitment. Perhaps part of it was that, growing up, I never truly heard that I could have a personal one-on-one relationship with Christ. It was always more like God was up there watching, ready to zap me every time I did something naughty. No one ever told me about knowing God personally, calling him Abba Father, Daddy.

Because of my rough home life, though, I began to rebel against my parents. I became wild. My older sister, Connie, was the good kid. But I had a *watch what I can do* attitude and did everything I could possibly think of.

When I was in high school, I would stay out as late and as often as I could. I decided it was okay to party and be wild.

After I graduated from high school, I went to Southeastern Oklahoma State University in Durant, Oklahoma. I was a freshman when my mother was diagnosed with breast cancer. She had a mastectomy and went through chemotherapy. It was too difficult for me to deal with the possibility of losing someone else I loved—especially after losing my brother. So I chose not to deal with it; I just ignored it. And I became committed to destroying my life. I drank all the time, partied all the time, never went to class. I had a stellar 1.69 GPA to show for it.

I was so miserable I kept hoping my wild lifestyle would bring me some peace—or at least help me forget my misery. It never did.

★ Brian

I attended high school and college in Beaumont, Texas. I graduated from Lamar University in 1984 and was commissioned as a second lieutenant in the U.S. Army. I chose the military because of the character and nature of the profession. My father, stepfather, uncle, and other family and friends had served in some capacity during World War II or Korea. I knew it was an honorable profession—and I wanted to be part of it.

I went to Field Artillery officer basic training at Fort Sill, Oklahoma, where I graduated in September 1984, and was sent on my first duty assignment with the Second Infantry division in the Korean demilitarized zone between North and South Korea.

Rod Fronk was a sergeant in my unit. And one day in late 1985, Rod said to me, "My sister-in-law is a perfect personality match for you."

"Oh yeah?" I said. But I didn't really think anything more about it because I figured he was joking. I can be a pretty serious person and Rod isn't—there's nothing serious about him. The man could be a stand-up comedian. So I wasn't sure what kind of gal he was trying to fix me up with.

About two months later I received a letter from his sister-in-law, Mel. I was surprised by the letter but thought that was kind of nice. Yet I wasn't sure how to respond to it, so I didn't.

She sent two or three more letters before I finally responded. And I sent back a very formal letter: "Dear Miss Collins . . ." At least it started that way! The rest of the letter I joked with her and kept it light. I figured I would have fun with our correspondence.

We passed several letters back and forth—mostly with me giving Mel a hard time about being from Oklahoma!

In late February 1986 I returned to the States to attend school at Fort Knox in Kentucky.

After school I headed to Fort Riley, Kansas, as my new assignment. By July I received a pass for a few days off, so I headed to Oklahoma to meet Mel.

★ Mel

In July 1985 my sister, Connie, was involved in a car accident, and my brother-in-law, Rod, came home at Christmas from Korea to see her. He brought home a photo directory of his unit in Korea.

One evening my high school friend and college roommate, Nikki Fitzgerald, and I visited Rod and Connie. We had been drinking heavily. I pulled out Rod's directory, and we began to look through it to pick out men we thought were cute.

I pointed to one guy. Rod said, "That's Brian Birdwell. He's my boss. He's a great guy." He started telling me all these great things about Brian, and Nikki and I looked at each other, impressed, and said, "Well, let's just write him a letter."

So we did. But we didn't hear anything back from him. So we wrote him again, and this time we received a response. His letter started "Dear Miss Collins." But then the rest of it was so funny! He talked about being 185 pounds of twisted steel and sex appeal, and that he lived in the last house on bad street.

We started writing back and forth, bantering, giving each other a hard time, and discovering our common interests—we both are big sports fans. Eventually we made contact by phone. One night he called me at my house, but I was out with friends. So my mother answered, and they ended up talking for forty-five minutes! When I arrived home, Mom told me about the conversation and said, "He seems like a really nice young man." But I thought, *What kind of guy calls my mother and talks to her before I've even met him?*

Finally, by July, seven months after I wrote the first letter, we arranged for our first meeting. He was on leave to visit his family in Texas, so he offered to pick me up and take me to Six Flags over Texas, an amusement park several hours from my house.

The day finally arrived, and I was so nervous! He pulled up in a pickup truck and got out to meet my family. He was wearing his Texas longhorn shirt, which was okay because I was wearing an official Oklahoma Sooner shirt! I presented him with a big Oklahoma-shaped cookie that had a longhorn emblem on it—which represented Texas—with a red circle and a slash through it. He was always teasing me about Oklahoma being substandard to Texas.

I knew he looked handsome from his photo in my brother-in-law's directory. But he looked even better in person! That made my heart race and my hands shake. Once I calmed down, I had a great time. It felt natural to be with him.

That began our relationship. By that time he was stationed at Fort

Riley, Kansas, and took leave to visit me every six weeks. And we still kept in contact by letter and phone. We had huge phone bills!

While I was attracted to Brian physically, what really attracted me was his stability. He had a strong belief in God and was a strong Christian. He didn't party or drink, and he really didn't know how much of that I did! He was the influence I needed to wake up and realize my lifestyle wasn't God's will for my life. At one point after talking about God with him, I thought, *I'm tearing myself down! I'm wasting my life, and I could be using it differently.*

So I stopped drinking and partying. I started going to church again and began to renew my relationship with the Lord. No one had ever had such a strong immediate influence on me. Brian's stability and faith drew me to him. He constantly encouraged me to renew my relationship with the Lord.

★Brian

By December 1986 I knew I was in love and wanted to spend the rest of my life with Mel. We discussed it and prayed about it. We both felt God's blessing. I understood the gravity of that decision—especially since my parents had experienced divorce. So at Christmas I proposed. We set the date for May 1987. I was twenty-five, and Mel was twenty.

Mel transferred to a college where she could be closer to her home in Davis to plan the wedding. While I knew her home life had been rough, she never told me the extent of how awful it was. One night she called me in tears.

I told her, "You get your stuff and move out. Go to your memmie's. We're not going to deal with this anymore."

★Mel

That phone call made a huge difference in my trust with Brian. I already knew I loved him, and I had spent a lot of time praying about our relationship and sought wisdom from Memmie and my mom. But with this phone call, I realized another important aspect to my relationship with Brian: I didn't have to worry about being hurt by Brian the way I'd seen modeled in my parents' relationship. Brian was sincere and rock solid.

We were married May 16, 1987, in Davis, Oklahoma, at the First Baptist Church. While it wasn't a military wedding, there were a lot of military people there. At one point, while standing at the altar, I looked over my shoulder and spotted two rows full of people in Army uniforms. A fear ran through me as I thought, *What am I doing?* It was so intimidating.

Even though my brother-in-law was in the Army, I really had no clue what to expect from marrying a soldier. I knew my sister would talk about Rod going to the field. He would be gone for two or three weeks. Then he would come home, and they'd have their normal life again. So I thought Army life would be Brian leaving for a couple weeks at a time, then coming home, and everything would be normal again. I didn't realize Brian would work twelve- and sixteen- and twenty-hour days.

Brian's stepfather, Pat, was an ordained minister, so he performed the wedding. I'll never forget one of the prophetic things he said during the ceremony. He said, "May God guide you in the bad that may darken your days and the good that lights your ways." We've certainly seen a lot of both.

Because Brian was stationed in Kansas, I transferred to Kansas State University. Being on such a large campus made me nervous because I was from such a small town and went to college in a small town. The worst part, however, was that two weeks after we were married, Brian was shipped to Wyoming for two weeks of training with a National Guard unit to act as their advisor. I was left alone.

Our marriage had the added stress of Brian's military lifestyle and my trying to finish school. Our biggest struggle was trying to find a church home. Finding a church to become connected with is difficult in the military because of the constant moving around. We were connected with the people at the church on base at Fort Riley because Brian worked with them. But it was also uncomfortable to worship when Brian felt he was at work rather than at church. So it was difficult to get connected with others who were there to experience community in a group of believers.

We went through a period where we didn't experience a lot of growth in our spiritual lives. We moved around a lot both in the States and in

One of the first pictures Mel saw of a young LT Brian Birdwell, shown here in Korea, 1984

LT Brian Birdwell leads a road march in Korea, 1985.

Mel and Brian Birdwell at their wedding in Davis,
Oklahoma, May 16, 1987

Brian tells two-week-old Matthew something very important, 1989.

Brian, Mel, and Matt, September 1999

CPT Brian Birdwell and CPT Gary Taylor
during Operation Desert Storm, Iraq, 1991

LTC Hope Jones, (then
COL, now MG) Virgil L.
Packett II, and Brian, then
Major, Birdwell in
Guatemala, February 1999

CPT Brian Birdwell and (then Major, now BRIG GEN)
Richard Formica in Hohnfels, Germany, 1993

MAJ GEN R. L. Van Antwerp, Brian, Matt, and Mel at Brian's
promotion to Lieutenant Colonel, November 30, 2000

COL Steve Shambach looks on as Mel pins on Brian's LTC rank.

LTC Brian Birdwell at his desk in the Pentagon, March 2001

Brian and Matt at the ACSIM annual picnic, September 7, 2001

Aerial view of the Pentagon following the terrorist attack of 9/11

The Pentagon following the terrorist attack—X marks the spot of impact.
Brian's office window is circled.

President George W. Bush thanks Dr. Marion Jordan, Director of the
Burn Center at the Washington Hospital Center, September 13, 2001.

President Bush as he leaves Brian's ICU room at the
Washington Hospital Center, September 13, 2001

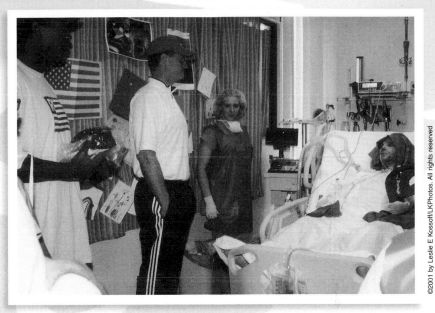

Washington Redskins Jeff George and Chris Samuels
visit Brian in the ICU, September 18, 2001.

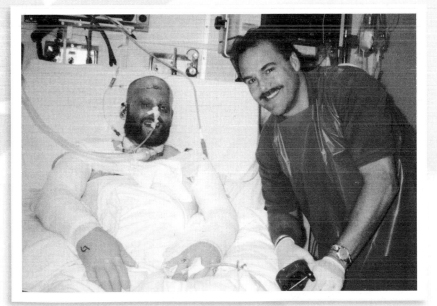

Retired Kansas City Chiefs kicker Nick Lowry
visits Brian in the ICU, October 5, 2001.

Brian, Mel, and then Chief of Staff of the Army, GEN (RET) Eric K. Shinseki, who presented Brian with a Purple Heart for wounds sustained on September 11, 2001

Brian administers the oath of re-enlistment to SGT Bigelow, October 16, 2001.

(Then Army Vice Chief of Staff, now GEN [RET]) Jack Keane and Brian visit at the Washington Hospital Center on Thanksgiving Day 2001.

Brian and Matt pose in front of the banner hung by the Birdwells' neighbors to celebrate Brian's homecoming, December 14, 2001.

LTC Brian Birdwell and MAJ John Collison in the hallway of the Pentagon, July 2002. John accompanied Brian to Georgetown on 9/11 and held his wedding band for him.

Brian at the Pentagon Memorial Chapel in May 2002, etching the names of Sandra Taylor and Cheryle Sincock, his coworkers who were killed on 9/11

Matt and Brian at the Olympic Torch Ceremony at the Pentagon, December 18, 2001

LTC Brian Birdwell's first day back at work at the Pentagon, March 12, 2002

Brian and Mel with the Ogletree family—Natalie, Mark, Avery,
and Aaron. Natalie prayed with Brian in the hallway
as he was being triaged on 9/11.

First Lady Laura Bush, President Bush, and Brian share a "Texan moment" at the White House prior to the Concert for America, September 9, 2002.

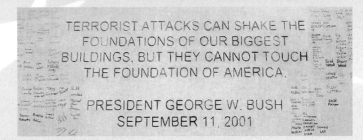

TERRORIST ATTACKS CAN SHAKE THE
FOUNDATIONS OF OUR BIGGEST
BUILDINGS, BUT THEY CANNOT TOUCH
THE FOUNDATION OF AMERICA.

PRESIDENT GEORGE W. BUSH
SEPTEMBER 11, 2001

A piece of the original Pentagon façade damaged in the attack. It was returned to the original quarry, engraved with President Bush's quote, and is now mounted in the Pentagon A Ring, 1st floor, Corridor 4.

President Bush and Brian exchange salutes in the diplomatic reception area at the White House, September 9, 2002.

Brian, Mel, and Bob Lepine of FamilyLife Ministries celebrating
the presentation of the Robertson McQuilkin Award for
Commitment in Marriage to Mel on June 22, 2002

Mel, Brian, and Matt
meet with Brit Hume
in Washington DC
prior to an interview
for FOX News Live
in February 2002.

NFL Hall of Fame
Quarterback Len Dawson
and Brian in the radio
booth at Arrowhead
Stadium during the Kansas
City Chiefs home opener,
September 15, 2002

Brian and Mel with friend and musician Dennis Jernigan in
Oklahoma City, September 2002

Brian visits with young burn victim Jonathan Smith at Regions
Burn Center, St. Paul, Minnesota, December 5, 2003.

Germany. I was able to connect with some Christian women. But by the time we moved to Germany in the early 1990s, I had given birth to Matt. I loved being a mother, but life was also extremely hard with a new baby. Brian was gone all the time, and my mom discovered that her breast cancer had returned. It was a miserable time in my life.

Mom had been in remission, so we'd thought everything was good. She was with me when Matt was born at Fort Riley in 1989, although the cancer had metastasized into her bones and she was having trouble walking. Two years later, after we'd moved to Germany, on June 12, 1991, Mom died. I was tired of losing people I loved. I was tired of feeling alone. To make matters worse, Brian was on duty constantly, and I didn't lean on God the way I should have. I didn't have much comfort during that time.

Soon after my mom died, the Army relocated us to Bamberg, Germany. God knew I needed help in the area of my faith, and he led me to Karen Mann, a wonderfully mature Christian woman. Our husbands were in the same unit, and she and I met at a wives' coffee. We connected immediately and became best friends. She taught me so much about everyday faith and helped me discover how to rely on God for strength.

Her teaching was important because in 1995 I would need to *relearn* how to lean on God for strength. That year became a spiritual turning point in my life.

★ *Brian*

Mel's Uncle Gary died in 1994. That was difficult for Mel. Her Uncle Gary had always held a soft spot in her heart because he had allowed her to mourn her brother's death and had comforted her.

Then Memmie began to have multiple strokes and became completely incapacitated. She died in 1995.

In the midst of dealing with Memmie, I was stationed at Fort Leavenworth, Kansas, where I worked full-time and attended graduate school at the University of Missouri–Kansas City. Basically Mel was a single parent; I was gone at least four nights a week between work and school. At that point I was assigned a job as a project officer in a combat developments division that I hated. It was a job with very little payoff. I was a major waiting for a pivotal school selection that would guarantee my career longevity in the military. I had been passed up for it earlier and was worried that if I didn't get picked for the Command and General Staff college, I would retire as a major with no opportunity for promotion or greater responsibility.

That year was stressful for us. Yet that was the year we made a conscious decision to become serious about our walk with God. We were Christians, but we had never gotten "down to business" with God. Between family challenges and work dilemmas too many situations were being thrown at us in which we felt helpless—so we said this was it. By 1996 we decided to stop playing "Christian" and actually start being Christians.

★*Mel*

We became involved in a church off base. I found a Bible study and began attending. I also started to keep a prayer journal. That kept me committed to praying for Brian and all the struggles he was going through. It was difficult to watch my husband struggle professionally—and feel helpless. I knew he felt the weight of being the main provider for his family, how daunting that was. Plus he had the additional pressure of school and a job he hated.

So I focused on my prayer journal; I wrote everything in it. I became serious about my prayer life. While praying separately and together didn't save us from the struggles, it comforted us. And it was a testimony as we watched God answer those prayers. Brian was transferred to Fort Lewis, Washington, and later in 1997 was finally selected for Command and General Staff college on his fourth and final consideration.

That year helped prepare me for the turning point in our marriage. We'd survived Brian's career stresses with the possibility of not being picked for the Command and General Staff college. We'd survived him being deployed to Desert Storm. All those circumstances brought us closer to each other. But in November 1998 Brian called me from his office on Fort Lewis and said, "I have to tell you something." What terrible words!

He was being deployed to El Salvador to work humanitarian relief after Hurricane Mitch. He was leaving in three days and would be gone for up to six months. I was devastated and cried the entire three days. I was upset that he wouldn't be home with me and our son every day. Deployments are common, but for some reason I can't explain, this deployment was tougher than the others.

While Brian was gone, I started doing daily devotionals and setting aside quiet times. I spent time writing in my prayer journal and focused on growing closer to God and to knowing more about him and the Bible. I learned just how much of a plumb line, a guide, the Bible is. And I craved it.

Brian returned from El Salvador in February 1999 and was transferred back to Fort Leavenworth to attend Command and General Staff college. Then in July 2000 he was assigned to the Pentagon, and we moved to Virginia. Five months later, in December of 2000, Brian was promoted to lieutenant colonel.

By this point we prayed about finding a church home as quickly as possible, and again the Lord answered our prayers. One day I was in the car running errands and listening to a local Christian radio station. The deejay announced that the singing group Phillips, Craig & Dean was giving a concert at Immanuel Bible Church that night. I love to listen to that group's music, so I decided right then we were going to attend the concert.

An interesting thing happened that evening. During the concert Philips, Craig, and Dean sang a song called "Freedom's Never Free," which talks about people laying their lives on the line for their country. While they were singing they were also showing video clips of the military. It was powerful.

While they were singing that song, Matt, who was eleven, started to sob uncontrollably. He asked me, "What if something like that happened to Dad?" I was surprised he was so worried, and I tried to reassure him. "That's not going to happen to your dad," I said. But I wondered, *He's never thought this before. Why is he so concerned?* It was almost as if he knew something.

After the concert we ran into some friends of ours we had known from Fort Leavenworth. They informed us they attended the church and invited us to come with them. We did the following week. It was a wonderful worship experience. And we knew immediately that God had answered our prayer for a church home. I'd never been in a church where the believers so love one another. It was a place where we could grow spiritually, where we could be connected to other Christians who were serious about God and living in a powerful relationship with him and others.

★ ★ ★

As we looked back over our lives while we sat for hours in the ICU, both Brian and I realized how God used the previous pain in our lives to prepare us for 9/11 and the difficult days to follow.

I remember clearly on the evening of September 11, sitting in the hallway at the hospital, praying. In my soul I felt the Lord speak. He laid out my life in front of me, and I saw all the pieces fit together, like pieces in a puzzle. He showed me how he had used the pieces of my life to prepare me to deal with this crisis.

In 2 Corinthians 5:5 the apostle Paul writes, "Now He who prepared us for this very purpose is God, who gave to us the Spirit as a pledge."

God reminded me of when my little brother, Tony, was injured and died, and I was shuffled from family to family while my parents stayed with him at the hospital. Recalling those days of my childhood helped me understand how Matt felt being away from us.

He showed me how he'd given me a godly grandmother, my memmie (I am determined to prove that somehow "Memmie" translates from Hebrew into "godly granny"). All my life she fervently prayed for me, loved me unconditionally, and discipled me. She was so dedicated to teaching her grandchildren about the love of Jesus Christ. God used her life of devotion to her family as an example to me.

God had also prepared me for dealing with grief and death through my mom's death. How greatly I missed her and longed for her to be there with us during those days. Brian said to me once soon after 9/11, "I wish your mom were here." All I could get out was a faint, "Me too" through the tears.

Then I thought back to my difficult childhood, filled with abuse and pain. I felt God say again, *I used those things to toughen you up so you could deal with things like this.* God's words brought such relief and blessing and comfort to me, to be reminded that God loved me so much that he would make sure my every need was taken care of in the darkest moments of my life. That brought me strength as I realized, *Okay, we can go through this.*

Throughout my life I have struggled with my personality. I've always wanted to be a quiet, sweet, submissive, agreeable person. And I'm just the opposite. I'm loud. I can be irreverent and say what I'm thinking before I edit my thoughts. But I'm also extremely loyal, a strong advocate.

However, through the dark days in the hospital as I took care of Brian and was his only advocate, I came to accept my personality with all its good and frustrating sides! I realized God made me this way for a reason. I had to be tough and durable—otherwise we would not have survived.

I became thankful that God made me assertive for that purpose. Brian and I recognized that no matter how tough things became, we were going to stay committed to each other and to God. There would be no divorce, there would be no giving up.

While God certainly didn't cause any of the pain to happen, he took that brokenness and those experiences from our past and used them to prepare us for what we were going through now. God took every experience and pain we'd had prior to that and reminded us that there is strength in trusting God and in using our past to comfort and help those around us.

ELEVEN

Tough Questions

JOURNAL 9/28/01

Today was the first time I saw his left arm where the unburned skin ended and the exposed muscle began. I think this is the first time I've been angry at the evil people who did this to him. What kind of evil could have done this to my precious husband?

★*Mel*

A week or so after Brian became coherent, he began asking questions. He asked if he still had a military career and if anyone had mentioned medical retirement. I had to tell him about the first night and the issues with Walter Reed. I was so glad I was able to assure him he was still a soldier.

He lay quietly for a few minutes as tears filled his eyes. Finally he looked at me and mouthed, "Thank you." That made up for the stress of that first night. We agreed we'd fight medical retirement with everything we could muster.

He also asked questions about his medical care. He was concerned that the correct amount of medication be given to him. He was unable to communicate clearly and was afraid the hospital staff would forget to do something important for his care. I tried to answer all his questions as best I could and told him that I was being truthful with him. I assured him over and over that we were in this for the long haul and we would get through it together. That seemed to bring him comfort.

I would look at my once strong, handsome husband, now reduced to a bundle of bandages and unable to do *anything* for himself, and I would become angry. Angry at the circumstance. Angry over the impact a killer's sin would have on my innocent husband, son, and me. Angry that I was forced to watch as other innocent family members and victims had to receive dire news day after day.

I read an article in the *Washington Post* on December 2, 2001, that summed it up:

[Victims] lost pieces of their skin, patches of their hair, parts of their ears, and entire fingers. They lost the use of their lungs. They lost days—many, many days—when instead of eating dinner with friends or raking leaves in the yard, they lay in bed, attached to blinking monitors.

That became our world. And it was so fragile. Between the infections, debridements, and surgeries there were many chances for him to die, even after we had so much hope. I felt as though we couldn't get past the all-clear mark.

I thought about Antoinette Sherman's needless death and the torture her family would endure for the rest of their lives.

I thought about the other patients who had to have parts of their bodies amputated.

Unfair didn't even begin to describe their circumstances. September 11 was a huge reminder that life isn't fair.

One day I went to the Post Exchange, a retail store on a military base or post, to buy a new pair of tennis shoes. While I was in the store, I felt this rising anger in me as I watched all these couples going about their lives as if everything was normal, as if nothing evil had happened. I wanted to yell at them, "Don't you know what happened on 9/11? How dare you have normal lives when the love of my life is fighting for his in a hospital bed!" While I knew it was completely irrational, I couldn't help how I was feeling. I was fueled by so little sleep and so much stress and anxiety.

It didn't help when I retrieved some mail from home and saw a letter from Tri-Care, the Department of Defense's HMO. The letter was addressed to Brian. It stated that Tri-Care believed a third party may be responsible for his injuries. I couldn't believe it. I thought angrily, *No kidding! But I don't think Osama bin Laden has Blue Cross.*

I was so angry, and I needed an outlet—and this insurance form was it! I read the form Tri-Care wanted me to fill out and return. They wanted a description of injuries. Asked, "How did the injury occur?" I wrote scathingly, *Soldier sitting at desk. Terrorist hijacked plane. Terrorist smashed plane into building. Husband critically injured.* I just underlined it all and mailed it to them. Soon afterward I got a call from one of their customer service representatives, who said, "Ah, ma'am, we're really sorry. You didn't have to fill that out." *You think? You looked at the initial form and read: "At the Pentagon on September 11." Chances are fairly good that my husband was part of that attack.*

I wasn't the most godly woman at that point, I'm ashamed to admit.

Yet in the course of the questions and anger, God continued to show up. Our church family was unbelievable. We were still relatively new to Immanuel and probably knew only twenty or twenty-five families. Yet the outpouring of love from so many people in the church was overwhelming to my spirit. They visited and prayed with us. They sang for us. They cleaned our house. They brought us food. They drove Matthew to and from the hospital on a moment's notice. They brought Brian a TV/VCR for his hospital room so he could watch John Wayne movies. They paid my cell phone bill. Whatever I needed, they made sure it was taken care of—even the least little thing. To them it didn't matter. If it was important to my family, it was important to them.

And there were others who cared for us. JoAnn Pendry, a friend of Jan Menig's, visited me. JoAnn's mother had been burned. She recommended that I read the book *Severe Burns.* She also brought me a gift package from Crabtree & Evelyn, filled with lotions and soap because she knew I was going to be at the hospital for a long haul. She told me about some of the things I was going to experience with Brian. As the days wore on, I discovered she hit the bull's-eye regarding surgeries and how everything would be two steps forward and ten steps back.

Nancy Fox, the social worker I had so disliked at the beginning of our relationship, also became a strong rock of support during those days. One day while we were sitting in the waiting room, she asked how I was doing. Then she confessed, "Mel, on September 11 I was so overwhelmed at the emotion of all the families, I couldn't let myself get emotionally involved with any of you. If I did, I knew I could not have gotten through *one* of those conversations, let alone *seven* of them."

We cried together and hugged each other. I realized that even people who didn't have family members directly injured from 9/11 were still hurting and processing the trauma, too. I appreciated her honesty. It helped me understand some of what she was experiencing and that Brian's injury affected her as well.

★ Brian

I'm not sure why, but I never thought, *Why me?* There was never a *Woe is me, Lord. Why did you let this happen to me?* I never considered any of that. I knew it wasn't because I was some tough Army guy. More so, it was because I knew evil people had made an evil decision. The Lord didn't will those planes into those buildings. Evil men made a choice to do so.

Every once in a while I played the *What ifs?* mind game. What if I had been running errands? What if I had talked to Mel before then? What if I had died? But I realized how futile that thinking was. The reality was that I was where I was—outside the men's room. When the plane crashed, I had no capacity to fight back. It wasn't even a matter of surviving based on any special Army training. It was purely God protecting me.

The only thing the Army did to help prepare me for this was to train me to be much more matter-of-fact. In the Army you know that everything has a purpose, even if you don't know it or understand. My Army training taught me to think, *Okay, here's the situation, and this is what we've got to do. It may stink, but let's get on with it.* Those of us in the military may say that in a very straightforward, nonchalant way. But it's not that we're not concerned about a crisis. We're just trying to process it, to bring as much order out of chaos without the emotional side taking over. And that same trained thinking helped me when I couldn't understand the reasons.

That's not to say I didn't ask God questions. I certainly did! I asked God on many occasions and in particular on those many long, sleepless, pain-filled nights lying in that bed, *Lord, why didn't you take me?* I was in so much pain physically, and I had a lot of mental anguish because of my inability to communicate other than spelling or mouthing words. Eventually we obtained a dry erase board to write things on—but even that didn't substitute for being able to fully communicate.

Mel struggled to understand what I was trying to say or do, and I don't think I succeeded well at communication. I thought many times about how it would have been better for the Lord to have taken me home when I was lying on the floor burning in the Pentagon.

I could have asked God, *You had the sovereignty to stop the plane. So why didn't you?* After all, I can see all the things he *didn't* allow to happen—for instance, the entire building didn't fall, the plane didn't hit a fully staffed wedge that would have killed more people—seeing how he knew what was happening all along. It seems as if God said, *I'm going to put these certain situations in play so that it can't be the worst.*

I also could have questioned, *If you did all those things, then why didn't you just not allow that to happen that day? Why didn't you make it rainy so the planes couldn't fly? Or bring snow or some other weird weather pattern?* Yet I think only the Lord can really answer those questions.

I've had people ask me, "If the Lord saved you, why didn't he save Cheryle and Sandi?" I guess in some ways people expect me to have some sort of survivor's guilt. I've not had survivor's guilt. The question is best asked of God, knowing he's going to answer that the day we get to heaven. But will we really be interested in the answer when we're already with him?

My point is that only the sovereign Creator of the universe can tell you why some things are allowed and some things aren't. I never thought what happened September 11 was the Lord's disciplining or punishing the nation—or me.

Evil people chose an evil course—and God allowed them, like all of us, to have free choice. But when that occurred, it brought America, as a nation, back to acknowledging God as our foundation.

I never thought, *Why didn't you stop the plane?* There were others who grew bitter toward God and asked, *Why did God allow this to happen?* But as Mel and I discussed it, our view was this: We are going through a difficult challenge. We don't really understand God's purpose in allowing this to happen. But we will be faithful.

Were there times when I just wanted it to be over? When I wanted the suffering to just stop? Oh yes. On the eighth or ninth day after coming out of the tank for debridement, I desperately wanted to die. In my heart and my mind I wanted to give up. I thought, *Why didn't you take me, Lord?* I begged God for death to come.

Still, even at that point I didn't think, *Why me?* While I didn't know why God had spared me, I knew it had to be for a reason. And I was determined to find out what that reason was.

★*Mel*

The worst day besides 9/11 came the day Brian's nurse walked into the waiting room and asked me to go to Brian's room. He had returned from a tank session and had a few moments before surgery. As soon as I cleared the curtain to his room he began reaching for me, sobbing. He begged, "Please, I can't continue to do this." He was in so much pain.

My heart was breaking. All I could say, "You have no choice. You have to do this. You have to keep fighting for Matt and me."

Yet even then, while I'm not sure why, I never asked God, *Why Brian? Why did this happen to us?* I did ask God, though, *Why did you spare Brian and not some of the others?*

I thought about those first days, when members of Antoinette Sherman's family spent hours with their pastor praying for her. Why didn't God answer by healing her and allowing her to live? Why did God choose to allow Brian to live and not her? Why did Antoinette have to die? Why did she live as long as she did, only to die? I thought, *Maybe to spare her the kind of pain Brian was experiencing.*

I thought about the other families who were directly affected by the terrorists' actions. People who normally would have been sitting right in the impact area, but, for some reason, weren't there that day. Either they had meetings, or they needed to run some errands. One lady told me, "I just had to go have a Slurpee. I don't even like Slurpees, but for some reason that day I just had to have one. So I went to get a Slurpee, and that's what saved my life."

There were a lot of days when I had to pray, *Don't allow me to succumb to fear and anxiety. Allow me constantly to renew my mind. Guide me through the day. Help me to show Christ to others.*

I didn't have answers. And I may never know on this earth. Sometimes there are no answers. God says in Isaiah 55:9,

For as the heavens are higher than the earth,
So are My ways higher than your ways,
And My thoughts than your thoughts.

I cannot explain the mind of God.

But I do know this: Every day I thanked God that he did spare Brian. God gave Brian to me twice.

One of the greatest ministry tools I had was music. So many times I'd put on my headphones and listen to music to escape my reality. I distinctly remember one day sitting at the end of the ICU hallway, staring out the window at the National Cathedral off in the distance, when my tape started to play the hymn "It Is Well with My Soul." It was probably the first time in my life that I actually listened to the lyrics penned by Horatio Spafford when his four daughters drowned in the Atlantic Ocean after a freak shipping accident:

When peace like a river attendeth my way,
When sorrows like sea billows roll;
Whatever my lot, Thou hast taught me to say,
"It is well, it is well with my soul."

Right then I told God, "This is *not* well with my soul, and I don't like the lot you've given me." I wanted Brian healed, home, and NOW! I had a nice little tantrum!

Through all my anger, I felt God's loving-kindness come through. I'd always heard people at church talk about God's *loving-kindness*— and I'd never quite understood what that word meant until that day in the ICU hallway. To me it meant the never-ending shower of God's perfect love. God has been merciful to me. He reminds me that this tragedy—9/11—hadn't been his plan either. But because of people's free will, they can choose to do evil rather than good. Yet I can choose to trust that he will carry me through this time.

How could I stay angry with God? I was blessed that Brian was alive. I had seen on television so many people whose spouses hadn't survived. What did I have to be angry about?

As time passed and I began to see and understand more of Brian's injuries, there were times when I'd become angry at the *people* who had committed this act of terror—cowards that they were, and in the name of their god no less! But ultimately I knew the fate they had chosen was far worse than anything I could ever have dreamed for them. I was able to work through that anger because I knew that the ultimate Judge, God, would be just, and he would hold accountable those who had caused such destruction.

TWELVE

Pressing On

JOURNAL 9/30/01
Saying good-bye to Matt was really hard. I cried. I feel so torn when he leaves, yet life is simpler when he's gone. I went to the waiting room to have some time alone with the Lord. . . . When Brian and I were alone he told me he was scared about what is scheduled to happen tomorrow with the tanking and surgery. He's worried about feeling the scrubbing they do; he wants to be knocked out. He's worried about whether he'll sleep tonight without having to ask for pain medication. . . .

★*Brian*

Won't this ever stop? I wondered almost constantly. Nothing seemed to help. The staff eventually put me on a PCA, where I could push a button and give myself pain medication.

I couldn't sleep. I could only lie on my back—which was burned. I couldn't move around because my body was so swollen and bandaged. There was only one position—and it wasn't comfortable. Nothing I did relieved the searing pain. I was unable to do anything for myself. I couldn't talk. I couldn't write because of the burns on my hands and fingers. I couldn't see well because of my infection and because I had lost my glasses at the Pentagon. While I had replacements, I couldn't wear them because of the burns to my face and ears. I couldn't walk well. I couldn't feed myself. I couldn't even go to the bathroom by myself! I lay in anguish—not just physically, but mentally. And I was scared.

I needed Mel to be with me as much as possible. I would open my eyes and immediately have to get a sense of my surroundings. Mel was always my reality check. I wanted her in my room when I was awake and when I came out of surgery. Because of the medication and the extreme pain, I couldn't focus mentally, and I was unable to understand what the staff did to me. When Mel was there she could explain everything to me or would at least hold my bandaged hand or rub my feet. Mostly, I just didn't want to be alone.

The times when Mel couldn't be with me, I could tell it was difficult for her to leave. There was an emptiness within me when she wasn't there. I knew my advocate was gone. She was the person who knew what worked and didn't work, what pain I felt and didn't feel. While the hospital staff changed each twelve hours, Mel was the constant who would always update the new nurse.

Mel was the one who made sure we continued whatever improvements were made in my treatments, including things I thought worked well for pain management.

★ Mel

I had a nickname. Some of the staff and the social workers from Walter Reed called me "The Pit Bull."

I knew I wasn't the kindest, most godly woman through a lot of this. But I also knew I had to do whatever was within my ability to ensure that Brian was well cared for and was as comfortable as possible.

One evening after one of Brian's surgeries, Dr. Jeng came into the waiting room to update me on Brian's status, then said, "Mel, you have to back off on the physical therapists. I don't think you should be in with Brian during that time anymore."

That frustrated me. I knew Brian was terrified of one of the physical therapists. When she worked with Brian, she seemed harsh and unsympathetic to his concerns.

I told Dr. Jeng, "I'll back off if she'll adjust the manner in which she deals with Brian. And *you're* going to have to explain to Brian why I can't be in with him anymore."

When Dr. Jeng left, I sat and stared at the wall. *I feel like I'm screwing up*, I thought, miserably. I didn't want to be a pit bull! But my job, as I saw it, was to be Brian's advocate—to do all I could to help him heal. He needed me, and I was trying to learn to do things for him.

Maybe I'm trying too hard.

I prayed again to seek God's guidance. While I wanted to do everything I could to give him the care he required, I realized I needed to let
him progress without pushing him. I also knew that he would never improve if he lost his determination. I wasn't going to allow that to happen, so I knew I had to take charge. I would try to back off on the
physical therapists. But it was a constant tug-of-war.

★ *Brian*

There was no rest for me. Nightmares took my mind captive as I slept.
They typically occurred when there was a change in my sleeping or pain
medication, which was often. They always revolved around either being
on fire, boiling, or experiencing intense heat. In one nightmare I relived
the entire experience in the Pentagon—except this time I died.

The worst recurring nightmare was that I was swimming in a perfectly blue, nice recreation center swimming pool while someone gradually turned up the heat until I was swimming in boiling water. I was
trapped in the center of the pool, being burned and trying desperately to
swim to the edge to get out. I splashed and flailed to get away from the
burning sensation. But the boiling water became hotter and hotter.
There was no escape.

★ *Mel*

I could tell when Brian was having a nightmare. He would hyperventilate, and his eyelids would twitch.

As soon as he started breathing heavily and quickly, I would wake him
to try to stop the dream. I would say, "Brian, you're having a nightmare.
You're safe. You're okay. I'm here." I would repeat those words while he
sobbed uncontrollably.

I couldn't hold or hug him because his arms still had no skin. My
words were the only way to console him. And that was hard. I could only
be so strong for him—especially when just watching his torture was tearing me up inside. I wanted it to stop! I wanted everything to become
normal again. I didn't think that was too much to ask! This was so unfair, so undeserved.

I would grab my Bible and read aloud. That seemed to soothe him—

and me. So many verses took on new meaning for us as I read. Like 1 John 3:2: "We are children of God, and it has not appeared as yet what we will be. We know that when He appears, we will be like Him, because we will see Him just as He is." It reminded me that we don't know what the future will hold for Brian or our family. I spent a lot of time praying that whatever the future held, I wanted it to glorify God. But mostly I wanted it to be easy. What human doesn't? Even though I knew from what we went through that there would be no such thing as an easy road on this trip.

And then there was Matt. I was overridden with guilt about leaving my son alone to fend for himself, even though I knew the Vances loved him unconditionally. Matthew had lived with Debbie Vance and her family for seven weeks by now. His family had been completely ripped from his life. He didn't know if his dad was going to live or die. Plus his dog, Hayley, was taken from him and sent to live with the Boykins. It was tough for him. He was enduring more than any twelve-year-old should ever have to endure.

I wanted to see him and spend time with him. But I was so torn! During my time with Matt I would think about wanting to be with Brian. I was so eager to be back in his room because I knew how desperately he needed me. And I'm ashamed to say there were many times when I counted the minutes until Matt would go back with the Vances so I could focus solely on Brian again. I had trouble knowing how to divide my time between the two people I loved the most. I asked God to show me how to manage my time with each of them.

Every time Matt visited he grew a little taller—until finally he was taller than I was. I felt as though I was missing out on his life . . . and that I was a failure as a mother.

There were also the day-to-day items I had to handle—bills, insurance, and household issues—that didn't disappear just because we lived at the hospital.

In late September Brian was ready to start on regular food. He had been fed through a feeding tube all this time, and he wanted Jell-O— and his morning Coke! *Well, my old Brian is returning,* I thought. I just shook my head. But deep down, I was thrilled.

He was starting to heal—even though it was a long, slow process. On October 1, I saw his unbandaged fingers for the first time since his surgeries. They looked like real fingers again.

By October 4 he was completely off the ventilator and breathing on his own. He received a plug for his trach and was able to talk to me now. It was exciting to hear that beautiful voice again. I was hoping his first words would be "I love you." Instead, they were "I'm tired."

After twenty-six days in the Burn Unit's ICU, Amy, one of Brian's physical therapists, announced that Brian was ready to be moved to step-down care. I was excited and scared at the same time. ICU was like a safe little cocoon; it had been our safety zone. What would we experience in step-down?

THIRTEEN

Moving to Step-Down

JOURNAL 10/8/01

*Well, this is the day. Mike is his nurse today. Day 27: The day we move
from ICU 4H6 to 3E32. It's exciting but scary. . . . Mike and I busily
began packing up all Brian's things and getting everything ready to go to
step-down care. Lord, I'm scared and nervous about this move. Guide us
through this process. Give me a peace that passes all understanding.*

★*Mel*

On the morning of October 8, Brian went to the physical therapy gym
on the Burn Unit rehabilitation floor, in step-down care. While he was
gone, I received word that we were moving out of ICU. I was busily
packing Brian's belongings when the nurse manager approached me and
gave me a lecture about how different step-down would be from ICU.
"Step-down is about Brian doing everything for *himself,*" she said.

I thought, *Man, these people are in serious need of compassion!*

Brian finished therapy, got settled into his new room in step-down,
and promptly began choking. He desperately needed suction to have the
mucus cleared from his throat and lungs. We were ignored.

This is going to stink, I thought, dreading the upcoming weeks. This
was such a huge shock and difference in the level of care.

ICU was great because his personal nurse was right outside his door.
No matter what he needed, that person would take immediate care of
him. In step-down the nurses each had four patients, so nobody was the
number-one priority. Brian was no longer going to have his needs met
instantly.

Fifteen minutes later I walked down the hall to find somebody to help
Brian. The nurses had been helping their other patients. I finally found

someone to help him. While he was being suctioned, I waited out in the hallway, pacing and praying. Dale Turner, the nurse practitioner, approached me and asked if I was all right.

"No, really I'm not," I said and started to cry. "I am so scared about Brian being down here. It was so much easier in the ICU. And this is the unknown."

"Well," Dale said in a compassionate tone that told me she'd given this speech many times before, "in my twenty-five years of working here, we've never had a patient die in step-down care. If he were still critical and near death, Dr. Jordan would not have allowed him to leave ICU. So practically speaking, he's going to be okay down here." I found her words reassuring because I thought, *Okay, I guess he isn't critical anymore.* But I still had to pray for God to give me strength and patience in dealing with the staff.

The next several days were trying for us. We had to readjust to new staff, new surroundings, new routines, new pain.

One of his physical therapists coldly informed me that Brian wasn't doing his facial exercises enough and that his face was going to scar because of it. Brian overheard her and became frightened. But being a soldier, he decided to step up to the challenge. He informed me that he intended to work extra hard in rehab.

During this time another patient's father stopped by and told Brian that he'd definitely face medical retirement. That was exactly what Brian didn't need to hear. After the man left, I closed the door, and we had our first cry together. It was devastating to see my tough guy, soldier husband sobbing. Fortunately, that night the staff permitted me to sleep in a recliner in Brian's room. I didn't feel comfortable leaving him alone with those worries swirling around in his head.

★ *Brian*
Wake up, breakfast, medication, physical therapy, lunch, nap, medication, physical therapy, dinner, medication, shower, dressing change, medication, sleep.

Then start all over again.

Day in and day out, it was the same routine.

I had surgery again two days after I moved to step-down care. Dr. Jeng put Integra on my arms, which is a synthethic material that would teach my skin buds how to act like dermis. He didn't anticipate any more surgeries for a while unless I caught another infection.

I grew more excited each day watching the seeding and skin buds grow from the grafting.

My bandages were still changed twice a day. But no more tank! Now I took showers. I sat in the stall while a nurse squeezed a sudsy washcloth filled with antibacterial solution on me. She scrubbed some of the areas that weren't burned. But for the donor sites and areas that still had no skin, the nurse just carefully let the soapy solution ooze from the rag onto me. Then she'd rinse me, help me stand, and dry me. The cleaning still stung—but it was paradise compared to the debriding sessions in the tank.

I was still dependent on others for simple tasks such as bathing or shaving. At times that was frustrating, because I wanted to do things for myself.

I established a rule. Visiting hours began at eight in the morning, and I informed Mel that when the clock struck eight, she was to be in my room, "standing tall!" She laughed and said, "Gladly!" I wanted her to be near me as much as possible.

On October 11, the one-month anniversary, there was a memorial service at the Pentagon. Colonel Rota escorted a group of family members from the hospital. I was relieved when Mel said she would rather stay with me to watch it on television. We watched the President say a few words, and I saw the ghastly façade of the wrecked Pentagon's west side, the side where I had faced death. The scene brought back all the wretched memories of that morning, and Mel and I sat and cried together. After the service was over, I confessed to Mel, "Sometimes I wish I hadn't survived because of everything I'm putting you through."

★ *Mel*

When Brian confided that to me, I tried to reassure him that it was a privilege to care for him and that my love for him was deeper than ever. That evening I returned to my hotel room and wrote in my journal:

To you, Brian, when someday you read this: It was heartbreaking to see you agonizing over how this is affecting me. You are the most amazing man I have ever known. You are strong, loyal, kind, respectful, and genuinely sensitive. The depth of my love for you is immeasureable. You are the most precious gift God has ever given, and it is a privilege to be your wife. I love you.

I knew I couldn't say those things without crying. So I wrote them.

The next day I walked into his room and knew immediately from the strange, familiar, putrid smell that his infection had returned.

During our devotional time together I looked up all the references to *suffering* in my Bible's concordance. We came to 1 Peter 5:10, which said, "After you have suffered for a little while, the God of all grace, who called you to His eternal glory in Christ, will Himself perfect, confirm, strengthen and establish you." After I read that, we both stopped and looked at each other. I couldn't believe this verse summed up our experience. This was a huge moment for us spiritually. I stood up and wrote out the verse on Brian's dry erase board that hung on one of his walls. We needed to read that verse every day.

After our study I prayed,

Lord, I know you are going to be glorified through this tragedy and you've used Brian to touch many lives. I know you will use him and his story in a mighty way to glorify you. What a privilege you have given him to be able to have such a powerful testimony in sharing Christ boldly. And while we look forward to our future together, I pray that you would heal him of this infection, that you would relieve his pain, and that you would bring him comfort as we walk through this suffering.

★ *Brian*

Back to surgery. The staph infection was back with a vengeance. It covered my entire arms, forehead, and ears.

During surgery, Dr. Jeng applied Acticoat to my forehead, ears, and arms. Acticoat is a gauze wrap that contains silver ion and other nutrients to help the healing. He also applied Xeriform, the mineral oil wrap, and medicated creams.

The night nurse was responsible for keeping the Acticoat wet because the water would help my body absorb the silver ion and other nutrients into my skin. After the nurse moistened the gauze, she would place chucks over my arms. These chucks were plastic-backed covers to ensure that the rest of my body remained dry while my arms stayed wet and cold.

Normally before showers and bandage changes I'd receive two milligrams of Dilaudid for the pain. After the showers and bandage changes I received two more milligrams of Dilaudid.

Several days after the surgery, it was time to remove the Acticoat. Minnie, one of the nurses, administered the shot of pain medication directly into my IV, walked me to the shower, and began to clean and remove the dressings. Everything came off without a problem—until she got to my forehead. She started to peel off the Acticoat . . . but my face came with it. It was stuck.

She tried to remove it gently, but it was so intensely painful that I started to tremble, then shake violently. She removed a quarter of the Acticoat, then stopped. My forehead was bleeding, and the blood was running down my face.

She ran to the nurses' station and asked a resident physician for permission to give me another two milligrams of Dilaudid. She administered it directly into the IV and waited for it to take effect.

I would have given anything not to have her remove any more, but I knew that was impossible. I told Minnie I was ready to try again.

She started to pull it again. But chunks of skin and tissue continued to peel off. I was still bleeding, and the Dilaudid wasn't helping! I started to shake violently again, and my tears mixed with my blood and streamed down my face. Minnie started to cry and ran to get the resident.

She returned to the shower with one of the residents, who took one look at me and gave the okay for another two milligrams of Dilaudid. I would have six milligrams running through me, a dosage close to making me unconscious enough for surgery.

Minnie waited for a few moments and began again. She was still crying and extremely distressed over what she was doing to me. While I no longer shook violently, I still trembled. I still felt the pain of her peeling off my forehead.

When the Acticoat was removed, Minnie gave me my bath. She tried to wash the area with a cloth. Then she wrapped cotton around my head, and dressed my arms and the other burned areas. We walked back to my room, where she helped me lie down on my bed.

I don't know if the Acticoat initially helped the infection. But in those moments of peeling it off, whatever good Dr. Jeng thought the Acticoat would do, it had just done twice as much damage. My face was now one big gaping wound, and the staph infection would get worse. Now it would move into my eyes.

★Mel

The next morning a hospital visit to the ophthalmologist confirmed that Brian had an eye infection. The ophthalmologist was concerned that the staph would damage tissue around Brian's eyeball. He prescribed liquid antibiotic drops, which seemed to help. I tried to aid the nurses when I could, since they were so busy with all their patients. So I swabbed Brian's eyes to clear the fluid and clean the mucus around them.

The worst part of the infection was on his forehead. Brian's face had only second-degree burns. But because of the infection, Dr. Jordan treated it as a third-degree burn. So Brian went back into surgery. Dr. Jordan shaved off Brian's forehead, basically peeling it to kill the infection. Then he grafted Brian's forehead, using cadaver skin just to close the wound.

When he came out of surgery, Dr. Jordan told me, "He cannot under any circumstance touch that graft."

The one night he was forbidden to touch his forehead was the night he decided he had to lay his arm there and potentially ruin the graft.

It was like wrestling a wild beast that night. I sat beside his bed, and every time he moved, I wrestled his arms down. Because he was so drugged, he didn't understand why I was being cruel and not allowing him to do what he wanted! The next night they brought in a sitter who watched him all night to make sure he kept his arms away from his forehead. The following night the nurses strapped down his arms. They placed Velcro on his bandages, then on the side of the bed. He was angry. "This is not a good plan!" he kept saying.

He played the woe-is-me part so well the nurses finally accommodated him. After three nights of not being able to touch his forehead, they removed the straps and allowed him to touch it. By that point, it didn't matter; the critical part was past.

Several days later Nancy Fox, the social worker, approached me, concerned about my well-being. "I think you're bordering on a mental breakdown," she told me.

I wasn't sure how to respond. I thought about several incidents that had happened just within the last few weeks and realized she was right; the stress *was* taking its toll on me.

I remembered the night the nurse gave Brian Ambien to help him sleep. She was supposed to give him five milligrams and gave him ten instead. In the middle of the night he was still awake and tried to reach one of the nurses. But he couldn't find the call button, which they had placed at his feet. For some unknown reason, he decided to get out of bed. Because he was so medicated, he couldn't get his balance and crashed onto the floor.

Then earlier in the week Debbie Vance had spoken with me about Matt. She was worried because he wasn't eating and had stopped applying himself in school. So I called and spoke with him. He admitted it was hard for him to focus. He was homesick and worried about Brian.

Then there was the incident with Brian, in which a nurse tried to teach him to eat with a prosthetic that Amy, one of his physical therapists, had made him. It was so painful and frustrating for him that he eventually threw down the prosthetic and dove his face into his Jell-O.

Then I thought about the day Dr. Jordan decided to cast Brian's arm to try to straighten it. He would straighten Brian's arm, cast it, and then a couple days later, cut out a wedge and straighten it more. While it would be painful, it would help his flexibility.

Because Dr. Jordan decided on the cast during surgery, when Brian recovered from the anesthesia, he took one look at the cast and went berserk.

He kept yelling wildly, "Why is there a cast on my arm? They broke my arm!"

I tried to calm him without much success. A resident physician, Dr.

Phil Ragland, was in Brian's room and couldn't understand what Brian was yelling because the plug in his trach, which helped him talk, wasn't in.

I tried to explain that Brian thought his arm was broken.

"What?" the resident said, looking distressed.

"Because of the cast, Brian thinks his arm is broken."

Finally Dr. Ragland understood and said, "Brian, no. Your arm's not broken. Everything is fine. The cast is to straighten your arm."

With all the medication in Brian's system, he was like a wild man. We couldn't get him to calm down and listen so he could understand. So they gave him medication to knock him out.

While waiting for the medication to take effect, Brian kept screaming and thrashing. I tried to talk to him, rubbing his feet to calm him down.

Finally Brian was able to understand that his arm wasn't broken. He calmed down, then drifted off to sleep.

I began to shake and cry.

Another extremely stressful event was the anthrax scare, which panicked me because they'd discovered anthrax at our main DC post office. A Kansas City reporter had written an article about Brian being a huge Kansas City Chiefs fan. In the article he'd encouraged readers to write to Brian. We were inundated with letters! It was wonderful for Brian—the outpouring of love and support from people all over the country. But I became fearful of touching the bags and bags of mail, afraid one of them would have anthrax on it. I obsessed over the anthrax. While I knew my thoughts were ridiculous, I couldn't change my thinking.

Then, when Matt was spending the night at the hospital hotel, he threw up all night. I started to cry, afraid Matt had anthrax. I was becoming hysterical and knew I had to do something to calm down. When Brian went into surgery, I drove to Walter Reed Medical Center to see an Army physician. I explained my symptoms: a cough, heaviness in my chest, night sweats, panic attacks, and my unusual exposure to large volumes of mail. The physician thought I should be tested for anthrax and started me on antibiotics as a precaution.

A few days later I received word that the anthrax test was negative. I was relieved.

★*Brian*

Physical therapy was the bane of my existence. There were times in step-down when the nurses would have to administer so much pain medication to help me through physical therapy (PT) that I would mentally float. There were other times when I left PT in tears, begging for God to let me die.

Because grafted skin has no flexibility, I had to work my body to force it to bend, stretch, move, and grip. Otherwise it would scar and become so stiff that I could be paralyzed.

The nurses would inject me with a shot of Dilaudid before I went to PT because the therapists were going to work my range of motion and "crank" on me, bending me the way my skin and joints should bend. I compared it to trying to bend a cracker without breaking it. It was taking leather and turning it back into skin again.

During my sessions I started with a paraffin wax treatment to warm up and loosen my skin and muscles and to soften the scar tissue. The therapist would wrap my hands with coban tape, then put the paraffin on me. While I knew it was hot, I couldn't determine how hot since I'd lost my sense of temperature with my skin.

Next the therapist wrapped my hands with Ace bandages to stretch my fingers to their maximum or to force them into a tight fist.

After fifteen minutes she removed the tape and bandages and began to work with each individual finger and joint. I would bend my fingers down and hold them for a ten-count, which was always painful.

Then I did exercises with my hands. One of my first days in physical therapy, the therapist gave me a stack of cones. All I had to do was take the cones off the pedestal and then put them back on. It looked simple; a three-year-old could do it. Except I couldn't.

The therapist would hold out my arms so I could reach the cones because my elbows were in a bent, locked position. I kept trying to grip the cones, to force my hands to do something I used to be able to do without thinking but now couldn't do, even with all the concentration I could muster. It was mentally agonizing. Here I was almost forty years old—and like an infant.

After that we exercised my arms, elbows, and legs. I worked on a weight system with pulleys. I used a stationary bicycle or a treadmill to peddle and stretch my legs. On occasion the therapist would strap a cane to my arms and then strap a sandbag weight around the cane, which I'd have to lift. That was truly painful.

One machine had screws placed above my head. The goal was to take a shape such as a triangle or a square, twist it off the screws from above my head, and twist it on a screw just below hip level. That way I was stretching my arms above my head and below my waist, twisting my wrists, and gripping the shape. I had to work to move all the shapes. I hated that machine!

There were also colored clothespins. Each color signified the amount of strength it took to open it. Yellow was easiest, then green, blue, red, and black. Black was the most difficult. I had to grip the clothespin, squeeze it to open, pull it off a metal bar, and set it down. After I removed as many as I could, I had to place them all back on the metal bar. I tried to make it a game so I could measure my progress. One day all I could do was yellow. With each passing day I could add a different color. However, I was never able to add the black until I was discharged from the hospital.

My worst day in PT was the day Ron, one of the therapists, placed me on a mat to work my right elbow and try to break up some of the scar tissue. I screamed through the entire session. Unfortunately Mel was outside the room, waiting for Matt to arrive, and could hear me screaming. When I returned to my room, I knew she had been crying.

The therapy sessions typically lasted a few hours. I was so exhausted from them that I would return to my bed and sleep soundly.

I became tired of being tired and hurting all the time. I became depressed and wondered, *How long is this going to take? When am I going to be normal again? When am I going to be able to do this for myself?*

All of this was part of a humility I was forced to endure. Sometimes I was angry with the staff members, who had never experienced what I was enduring. I was a lieutenant colonel in the United States Army. I had been through hell—wars, deployments, bombing, and being shot at. I'd been through more in life than what they'd seen. When they called me a whiner and a moaner I found that insulting. I didn't need a twenty-five-year-old physical therapist to tell me what a baby I was. I knew what I was going through. I understood very clearly what was happening to me and how rough a mission I had been given.

★ *Mel*

In late October while Brian was in PT, I saw Dr. Jordan in the hall. He stopped me and said, "Mel, I'm concerned about Brian. He really needs to be working his hands constantly. If he doesn't, they'll scar to the point that he'll never be able to use them again."

I assured Dr. Jordan that I would mention that to Brian, which I did. Something in our conversation must have sparked some challenge within Brian. After that he started to turn a corner in his recovery. At lunch he opened his own milk carton! He told me that while he still dreaded PT, he didn't fear it anymore. He was fighting the fight!

Now it was time for him to see Matt again. In the twenty-six days Brian was in ICU, Matt had visited Brian once. He would sit in the waiting room every once in a while. But mostly he stayed at the Vances or went to the hotel where I was staying. Brian started to bug me about getting Matt to visit. But every time I would ask Matt, "Do you want to visit your dad?" he would say, "No." He was afraid to visit because he didn't know what he would encounter. The first time scared him enough that he didn't want to do that again.

Soon after Brian received the cadaver skin graft on his forehead, he told me, "Enough is enough. Get that kid in here. I don't want to hear any more about Matt not wanting to come. You tell him he's coming. This is an order, so he can stop sniveling and get down and see his dad."

I gave Matt his orders. His eyes almost bulged, he became so terrified. But he could see this time we weren't backing down. So he said, "Okay, I'll go in and see Dad."

Matthew walked in, took one look at Brian's forehead covered with the cadaver skin and the infection, and gulped. The sight of Brian's face horrified him. And Brian was extremely thin, less than 130 pounds, compared to his normal 168 pounds. It was a shock. We cried together. I told Matt it was okay to be scared. Then I tried to joke with him about how much Brian resembled Bert from *Sesame Street*.

Matt said, "Dad, whatever you need, you just have your nurse call me. I'll be over here in a second, day or night." From that point on, he felt more comfortable visiting Brian—still not every day but more frequently.

★ *Brian*

I received word from General Van Antwerp during one of his frequent visits that I was to receive the Purple Heart medal. Since I was unable to attend the official ceremony, General Eric Shinseki came on October 24 and presented the medal to me in the hospital. Even in the hospital room the small ceremony was moving. I felt honored to receive the prestigious medal as General Shinseki pinned it to my pillow.

As with President Bush's visit, I had just been prepped for surgery to autograft my arms. After General Shinseki left, Dale, the nurse practitioner, found a photo of the Purple Heart on the Internet, printed it off, and pinned it to my hospital gown so Dr. Jeng would see it in surgery. He thought that was great!

This was one of the toughest surgeries. Dr. Jeng grafted most of my arms with skin taken from my upper thighs. For days I had trouble walking. Every time I moved my legs the exertion caused the blood to rush to the donor sites. It felt as though someone was stabbing millions of needles into my legs.

At some point I just wanted the pain to stop. I religiously watched the clock for my next round of medication. Then as the grafts began to heal, the intense itching started. A nurse would administer a shot of Benadryl every six hours. I could have one shot every six hours, and I watched that clock like a hawk.

In the beginning of November I had Z-plasty done to my eyes. My face was contracting and scarring, which was pulling my lower lids down and drying out my corneas. Dr. Jordan cut an incision in the shape of a Z and put a small piece of skin from my abdomen in the incision to release the contraction so my eyes could close. Then he put a tight cotton roll on top of the graft and stitched the roll into the skin. My eyes would be closed completely for eight days, then the roll could be removed. Before that, every night Mel would put a special medicated cream along my eyes to keep them from drying out while I slept, since my eyes didn't close.

Mel told me Matt would walk by when I was sleeping and tell her, "Mom, he's sleeping like a dead person. Go close his eyes."

★ Mel

November 3. Brian's fortieth birthday. This certainly wasn't how I'd imagined spending the milestone day, but I couldn't complain—he was alive. He looked into the mirror that morning and said, "I think I look pretty good for a guy who just got run over by a 757."

Our friends Dennis and Joyce called to say they wanted to visit and asked what food they could bring for the birthday celebration. "Taco Bell!" was the reply. Brian had been craving food from Taco Bell and his usual Coke. So that evening we crammed into Brian's room, ate Taco Bell food, and watched a college football game on television.

There was a missing piece to the celebration, though—Matt. I was tired of Matt not being with us. He was still being shuffled between friends and family, and I knew I could no longer spend my time moving him around. It wasn't fair to Matt. And I couldn't focus on helping Brian if I had to continually find somewhere for Matt to live. So I finally decided he would come to the hospital and live in the hotel with me.

So ten weeks after September 11, Matt joined us as a family again. Everyone in the hospital got to know him. He was the little twelve-year-old running around everywhere!

It felt good to have Matt staying with me. We brought his Play Station from home and hooked it up to the TV. We were able to work on his schoolwork while I did laundry in the hotel's small laundry room.

★ Brian

I could see the hospital's MedSTAR helipad from my window. *That's not a good sign*, I thought once—while I was in a good mood and could laugh. I told God, *Okay, Lord, my office at the Pentagon overlooked the helipad. Now my hospital room overlooks the helipad. What are you trying to tell me?* Those were the moments when the pain would subside enough for me to have a sense of humor. Of course, that, as everything else, wouldn't last.

I'd been in the hospital almost two months when Dr. Rhodes, my pain management physician, entered my room.

"Good morning, Brian," she said. "How are you doing?"

"Not bad, this morning," I told her.

"I'm glad to hear that. Brian, you're starting to heal nicely. While you still have a long road, you're doing much better handling the pain. We're going to begin lowering the amount of pain medication you are receiving."

"Whoa! Hold on," I told her. "What do you mean we're going to lower my pain medication?"

"It's understandable that anyone on the amount and type of medication you've been on, for as long as you've been on it, would struggle with an addiction to it."

"What are you saying?" I asked, afraid of what her next words might be.

"That's where you are right now. Brian, you are addicted to the pain medication."

I didn't like hearing that. My feeling was that I'd already been through enough trauma. I didn't want to have to tolerate more pain, too.

"So when I come out of surgery, I have to deal with the pain? Is that what you're telling me?"

"There are other options we're going to explore. Drug-free options."

I was angry. I could tell the decision had already been made. This was reality—and I was just going to have to deal with it.

FOURTEEN

Waiting on God

JOURNAL 10/12/01
Lord, you know I'm anxious about what the future holds for Brian.
I know he's eventually going to be fine—I'm just a little scared about the
journey there.

★*Mel*

In John 16:33 Jesus says, "In the world you have tribulation, but take courage; I have overcome the world." It's a guarantee that everyone will, at some point in his or her life, experience hardship and pain. Those are the moments when we desperately need to lean on God's strength.

There wasn't a day that went by while Brian was in the hospital that I wasn't praying and trying to center myself in God. Almost every breath I breathed was a prayer. The apostle Paul says to "pray without ceasing" (1 Thessalonians 5:17). That was me. Some people call that a crutch; I call it a lifeline. I think I prayed more in the three months Brian was at Washington Hospital Center than I had prayed in my entire life.

We went from a normal life to absolute chaos and the unknown. Every step we took felt as though we were stepping off a cliff. We learned every day about stepping out in faith.

There were so many times when all we could do was trust God. I would hear him speak in the recesses of my mind and heart. He would say, *I have this under control. I don't need your help in this. Just follow the path I lay out for you.* Those were such difficult words to hear because I like to have control.

One night as I sat in Brian's room listening to a CD, I heard a song performed by the worship leader Dennis Jernigan. It was titled "The Point of Grace." Dennis captured exactly what I was feeling and experi-

encing. It was as if God picked out this song specifically for me to listen
to during those days:

When the fire of life leaves you so dry
that your eyes have no tears left to cry;
when heartache leaves you wond'ring why.
Or wond'ring how you will survive!
When you've grown too tired to run the race;
find your strength is gone with-out a trace;
when you've reached that lonely desp'rate place;
you have reached the point of grace!

I will meet you there where your striving ends!
I will hold you there in My embrace!
You will find the place where true joy begins
when you've reached the point of grace!
When you've reached the point of grace!

When your hopes and dreams begin to fade;
disappointment clouding all the plans you've made;
feeling lonely, broken, and afraid;
it seems so long since you have seen the light of day!
When it seems like ev'ry trial you face leaves you one step closer
*   to the place,*
where you fall away or reach for My embrace . . .
Child, you have reached the point of grace!

Just let go and you will see.
Just how mighty love can be!
Child, your greatest strength is when you're weak,
looking up from your brokenness to me!

I knew about brokenness: never leaving the hospital, looking at my
precious husband whose body had been so physically devastated, not
knowing if all the dreams and plans we'd made for the rest of our lives
were now gone. Just being at the hospital all the time was oppressive.

There's not a lot of joy coming out of a burn unit, so it was difficult at times to maintain a positive perspective.

I learned quickly that the only way I was going to make it through this experience was to depend totally on God. I knew this was way bigger than anything I could control or make better. Those were the times when God would gently remind me of 2 Corinthians 12:9-10:

And He has said to me, "My grace is sufficient for you, for power is perfected in weakness." Most gladly, therefore, I will rather boast about my weaknesses, so that the power of Christ may dwell in me. Therefore I am well content with weaknesses, with insults, with distresses, with persecutions, with difficulties, for Christ's sake; for when I am weak, then I am strong.

Okay, maybe I wasn't well content with weaknesses, with insults, with distresses, but I was definitely game for depending on God!

More than any other time in my life, this experience personalized my relationship with Christ. It became a deeper, richer relationship.

On September 11 when I found out that the Pentagon had been hit, I had gone immediately to the Bible verses that had always been important to me, such as Psalm 91—the same psalm that Natalie read to Brian in the Pentagon. As I read those verses, they took on a meaning I had never realized. Now I read them again. For the first time in the hospital the words of the psalmist caught my attention. The psalmist talks about God's angels spreading their wings over us to protect us. I couldn't get through reading it without crying because I realized that God was talking to Brian and me. He had done this for us. He had provided this protection for us.

It seemed as if every psalm I read talked about being carried in God's hand. And I knew that was exactly where Brian was—I could visualize it.

Before every surgery Brian was so afraid. So we would pray together. I felt God's presence descend upon us during those times. It was such a strong feeling that he was with us, so strong that, deep down, I knew everything would turn out all right in the long run. It would simply take time.

★ *Brian*

Mel continually stood by my bed and read the Psalms and other passages of Scripture to me. Hearing words from the Bible had become even more important to me in such a time of emotional and physical pain. I wanted Mel to read to me as much as she could. It seemed as if every psalm she read talked about God carrying me in his right hand and protecting me. I felt God was talking directly to us. Through the Bible he was telling us that he protected me from my enemies and that justice would be his. It was comforting and powerful to hear her read, to be reminded of the great God we serve.

After Mel read 1 Peter 5:10, she wrote it on a dry erase board and hung it in my room so we could be reminded of that promise every day: "After you have suffered for a little while, the God of all grace, who called you to His eternal glory in Christ, will Himself perfect, confirm, strengthen and establish you." That was not only a promise God made to us spiritually; it was a promise he made for me physically. I don't know why the Lord kept me alive. Only the Lord can answer that question. But he kept his promise to me. While I may not be physically the same as I was before that day in the Pentagon, I am certainly a much stronger and better Christian after this experience.

Our marriage is also stronger. I am fortunate to have a spouse who understands the gravity of our wedding vows. She definitely had to deal with the "for worse" and the "in sickness" part.

We have been through the refiner's fire as the Bible discusses in Zechariah 13:9. The Lord says,

"I will bring [them] . . . through the fire,
Refine them as silver is refined,
And test them as gold is tested.
They will call on My name,
And I will answer them;
I will say, 'They are My people,'
And they will say, 'The Lord is my God.'"

We've been tempered spiritually by the fire we've gone through. We were placed under the heat and the fire, and we've emerged a stronger product.

There were so many days when I would lie on my bed and ask God, *How much longer until I can be normal again?* The answer came on November 5, when I finally felt well enough to feed myself all my meals, to put on my pants, to open the bathroom door, and tie my robe. Things I had taken for granted so many times and so few months before!

I was also able to go outside for the first time since 9/11. I walked, with Mel pushing a wheelchair next to me, down to a small courtyard. Once I arrived I was tired—but I was there! I was so excited to be outside again, to be able to look up at the blue sky that I hadn't seen for two months.

As I gazed up at that beautiful clear sky, I said simply, "Thank you, God, that I'm still here." I had waited on God, and he proved faithful. The great Creator, mighty God knew and cared about *me*. I stood breathing in the fresh air and wondering in awe about God's love for us.

That brief glance of the sky gave me a renewed sense of purpose. I knew Christ had saved me from that fire. I believed my life was spared because I still had a mission to complete. Ever the soldier, I knew my commander, God, would reveal my mission in due time. But until then I had to continue to wait and be faithful in doing my part to heal.

Through this experience Mel and I discovered the things that were truly important. They are not connected to our careers or even receiving the Purple Heart—although those are wonderful things. The important things of life are how we live our life in our day-to-day relationships. We learned how vital it is to "stay the course" as a Christian through the "little things" so that when and if the "big things" come, you have the peace and endurance to walk with God through them.

That's not to say we didn't have our moments of frustration and outbursts of anger. We're Christians, but we're still human! There were times when both Mel and I said things out of our pain to other people or to each other that later we felt sorry about. But we felt God give us strength to endure the many torturous indignities and to be able to somewhere along the line still give thanks for delivering us.

Even when I was in pain, I tried to be respectful of other people, knowing they were overwhelmed with all their work as well as trying to process their own grief and shock from 9/11. Just a simple thank-you went so far. One nurse, Minnie—the one who had unintentionally peeled off my forehead while trying to remove the Acticoat—said to me, "You know, Brian, I come in here and do horrible things to you, and I leave and you tell me thank you!"

Those are the important things we found about this life: Never take anything or anyone for granted.

★ Mel

I believe in prayer. Throughout this entire ordeal, I witnessed signs of God's sovereignty and power. He answered my prayers each time I prayed, although it was in his timing. I came to believe that if God had brought us this far without help from me, he could handle it the rest of the way. That understanding brought many nights of peace.

I never felt closer to the Lord than I did during these months. Our relationship deepened and intensified. It played such a crucial role that many times I felt as though I could reach out and physically touch Jesus Christ. During the darkest moments of despair, when I hit what I thought was the absolute bottom, God comforted me in unexplainable, supernatural, indescribable ways.

Not that I hadn't prayed a million times in my life or ever had a prayer answered prior to September 11. But never before this event had I felt God's presence so near as I did while Brian was in the hospital. So many nights I would sit at the foot of Brian's bed, and while rubbing his feet, I'd pray over every single part of his body, starting at his head.

God, heal his ears, his face, his head, his neck, his chin, his shoulders, his arms. . . .

And little by little God did.

For example, one day while Brian was in ICU, one of the nurses approached me with a smile on his face. He said, "I was giving Brian a bath today and started scrubbing what I thought was a wound. But it's skin that is healing—and it's healing well! It shouldn't be healing this quickly."

I smiled and said, "That would be a God thing. God is doing that."

Each time a "God thing" happened I thought, *This is all going to be okay.*

We learned to savor the small steps. I thanked God for his goodness to us and wrote my praise throughout my journal so I would always re-member. Every time I wrote a prayer request in my journal, later I no-ticed I was writing my praises for how God had responded. It was still a long process, and some days it felt as though God wasn't working quickly enough, but he *was* still working. He knew Brian's needs better than we did.

In one journal entry I wrote:

Your Word tells us that when we can't find the words to pray, that Christ intercedes for us. I rest in that truth when all I want to do is demand and plead for Brian's immediate healing. Thank you for easing his pain yesterday. I pray for another day of relieved pain and a day to praise and glorify you. Strengthen me. Hold me up through this as I am so weak and stumble easily. When I get the least bit frustrated or tired, I snap.

Even when I didn't know how, I knew God was working. There were times when I didn't understand many things, and many times I couldn't see God working. But he promised he would bring us through, so I trusted that he would. I never doubted Brian was going to make it. While it was scary, I always had a peace in my heart that he was going to come home again.

Every year on Thanksgiving morning our church holds a worship ser-vice. Brian and I discussed how we would like to attend if Brian was strong enough. This would be the first time he had been out of the hos-pital, not counting the courtyard, since 9/11. Since Brian was recuperat-ing well and the infection was under control, Dr. Jordan authorized a day pass to leave the burn ward on Thanksgiving.

I dressed Brian, put him in a wheelchair, and pushed him to the lobby. I had to leave him with a security guard while I retrieved the car. Then the guard and I gently helped Brian lift his legs and bend down to get into the car. The real challenge was getting his seat belt on him since it wrapped around the donor sites and caused irritation.

How thin and frail he looked as he sat in the car. I thought, *This must be a preview of what Brian is going to look like in old age!*

We drove to our church, where our friends John and Gene Hall were waiting at the door. They walked us down to Pastor Jack Elwood's office so Brian could sit and rest before the service started. We visited with Jack, Pastor Steve Holley, and others who stopped by to say hello.

Just before the service began, we walked to the sanctuary. Few people from the church knew who Brian was before September 11. On September 12 during the prayer service, they displayed Brian's photo on a screen and talked about him in-depth before praying for him. Since almost fifteen hundred people were attending that evening, everybody became familiar with Brian.

As we walked through the lobby, though, nobody recognized him. Of course he looked *nothing* like that photograph. He looked like a sickly, stiff old man. He was wearing a hat, was hunched over when he walked, and had this crusty stuff—the skin grafts—all over him. A couple people peered at him as if to say, *What happened to that guy?*

John and Gene saved a seat for us in the second row on the far left side of the sanctuary. As the service began we slipped into our pew, pretty much unnoticed. Matt sat on the front row directly in front of us.

The service started with some worship songs. Leah Little, a member of our church, spoke about her recent missions trip to Ghana. Afterward, a pastor from Ghana spoke about what was happening in the church in his country. Then Jack Elwood stood and said, "We have been praying for Lieutenant Colonel Birdwell. JT Walker, the pastor of community outreach, Angie Ruffin, and I went to the hospital and interviewed Brian recently. We made a video of that interview and would like to show it to you."

As the video played we looked around the sanctuary and saw many people crying. Afterwards Jack went to the podium and said, "When we made the video we had no idea that Lieutenant Colonel Birdwell might be able to attend this service with us. Would you do me the honor of welcoming a good soldier of Jesus Christ, Lieutenant Colonel Brian Birdwell." The audience gave an audible gasp, and eleven hundred people rose to their feet for a long and passionate standing ovation. We were overwhelmed by their support. Brian, Matt, and I were crying and hugging. What an incredible tribute. The love that the church has poured out on us has been tremendous. These people, most of whom we'd never met, loved us simply because Christ asked them to.

After the service it seemed as if every person in the sanctuary stopped by to say hello. By the end Brian was exhausted—but happy.

★ *Brian*

We planned to drive by the Pentagon on the way back to the hospital so I could see the damage. As we drove closer to the building, I noticed that everything was cleaned up. There was no debris, no wreckage, no rubble. While there was a huge slice where my office had been between Corridors 4 and 5, it just looked like a big parking lot.

We originally planned to drive up to the building. As we got closer, however, I changed my mind. I told Mel, "No, just keep going. Let's get back to the hospital."

After having had that amazing experience at church, seeing the Pentagon seemed insignificant. The Pentagon would still be there later. I'd seen the photos. I just no longer felt the need to see it.

We continued to focus on regaining my strength and on overcoming my addiction to pain medication, as well as learning how to work through the pain and the frustration of my setbacks in physical therapy. That was our world. Any television I watched consisted of anything that didn't remind me of 9/11—usually ESPN. I already had enough reminders of that day; I didn't want to know anything more about it.

When I got to step-down care in October, the Afghan War had started, so we watched the news. But since the replays of the collapse of both towers of the World Trade Center had occurred while I was in intensive care, I didn't know the results of that attack. I only remembered that they had been hit. Mel and I had never discussed it. Our concerns had been centered around my surgeries, physical therapy, and pain.

So in December, when Mel turned on NBC news, I saw for the first time the replay of the video of the burning buildings. I watched as the second tower with the tall antenna on it began to drop and twist a bit. I lay there, thinking, *What happened?*

I looked, startled, at Mel, who just then realized I never knew what had happened in New York. When I had stepped out of my office to go to the men's room, the towers had been hit, but the collapse hadn't yet occurred.

It was now three months later, and I was learning what had happened to the World Trade Center towers. Mel said, "They don't exist any more. They're just big piles of rubble. The reporters believe more than three thousand people were killed."

I was stunned. It was as though what I had seen wasn't real.

FIFTEEN

Going Home

JOURNAL 11/14/01

Lord, this is difficult. I feel very distant from you. Change me, Lord. This is so much more than I can do. Only you can change me. Prepare me for this and carry me through. I am a mess and feel as though I can't cope any longer. Lord, help me to cast my cares on you. I need to give everything to you. Forgive me for all that I've been holding on to and dwelling on instead of renewing my mind constantly to the obedience of Christ. . . .

Brian's healing is amazing. It seems as though every day his strength improves by leaps and bounds. We are praying for one more surgery (a contracture release) and then his discharge. The plan is to move to the hotel and he'll go over to the burn center for PT every day.

★*Brian*

On December 5, 2001, nearly three months after 9/11, I was discharged from the hospital. I had spent twenty-six days in the Burn Unit's ICU and eight weeks in the Burn Unit's step-down care. I received more than thirty surgeries and countless hours of debridements and physical therapy. I was *more* than ready to be released.

I didn't go straight home, however. I moved into the hospital's hotel with Mel and Matt for a week because I was still doing physical therapy every day and we needed a transition period to become reacquainted with life outside the Burn Unit.

That time was good for us to make the transition because if something went wrong, all Mel had to do was put me in a wheelchair and roll me the five-minute walk to the Burn Unit. Fortunately, nothing major happened. So we decided it would be better to go home and have a seminormal life. Since I still had physical therapy five times a week, I would commute back and forth.

On December 14 I went home. It felt almost like being released from prison! Other than being outside in the courtyard or out for the Thanksgiving church service, my surroundings had been the same for the past three-plus months: my room, the hallway, operating room, shower room, physical therapy room. Day in and day out, the same.

It was like a novelty staying at the hospital's hotel. But the real celebration came when Mel was able to take me home. I would go up my stairs, watch my television with my cable selections versus the hospital cable selections, open my refrigerator, and eat what I wanted instead of the hospital food. I couldn't wait to get home!

★ Mel

When Matt and I heard that Brian was going to be discharged, we went home and unpacked and decorated the Christmas tree. Brian had a white Christmas tree that he adored that we *had* to put up every year. In reality, it was hideous. This year, though, it was a beautiful tree simply because it was his.

We were so excited about finally being home. It felt as though our lives were going to be somewhat normal again.

Our next-door neighbor, David Hamilton, offered to ask the Arlington County Police Department to give us a police escort home. We laughed but declined; we wanted Brian's homecoming to be low key. We didn't want anybody to know we were coming home.

When we arrived at our home, however, we saw a yellow ribbon and a huge sign—Welcome Home, Brian—that our neighbors had hung on the tree in our front yard. Our neighbors were waiting to greet us in front of our house. David helped me get Brian out of the car and gave him a big but gentle hug. We took some photos, then went inside. Finally it was just us. It was wonderful to have family time and just be quiet together.

The first evening we were so exhausted all we could do was sit on the couch and watch television.

We didn't have a lot of time to kick back, relax, and look back over the last three months because the ordeal was just beginning all over again. I thought I would be overly emotional about the homecoming. But it was more of a relief—until reality set in. I began to think, *How am I going to take care of Brian by myself? How am I going to get him up and down the stairs to bathe him? What if I hurt him?*

The responsibility for Brian's care rested completely on me, and he required constant attention. I was going to do all of his wound care. If he became ill, it was my responsibility to take care of everything. The nurses trained me on the proper way to work with his bandages and medication. I had been helping them work with Brian in the step-down unit anyway, so that wasn't new to me. My biggest concern was about doing it alone. It was time-consuming—and a lot of hard work!

If I had a problem or a question, I couldn't just step into the hallway and ask someone. I had to figure it out or make a phone call.

His first bandage change took me an hour and a half. With practice I finally mastered it in forty-five minutes.

For the first two weeks Brian had physical therapy five days a week. After Christmas it was reduced to three days a week and continued for the next three months.

On Brian's physical therapy days, I would wake at six o'clock and spend some quiet time with God. I would read my Bible, write in my journal, and pray. I recognized that time spent with God was going to be my lifeline.

I woke Brian at seven o'clock and helped him dress since he was still unable to completely dress himself. Then I would feed him breakfast, give him his medicine, and discuss his schedule for that day.

After breakfast I brushed his teeth, shaved him with an electric razor, and put his socks and shoes on him. Then we waited for the MedSTAR drivers to pick him up to take him to physical therapy. He usually left around nine o'clock and returned home by twelve-thirty.

I bought a bag for him to carry his medication, cell phone, patient ID cards, and other essentials to physical therapy. The brand name of the bag was Body Bag. Brian thought it was hilarious that I bought him a body bag.

While Brian was at therapy, I homeschooled Matt until Brian returned. We would have lunch as a family, and then I would focus solely on Brian while Matt continued his schooling on his own.

Because physical therapy exhausted Brian, I would give him his medication, let him sleep for an hour or so, and return to working with Matt.

When Brian awoke, he and I worked on his physical therapy. I would "range" him, which included bending and straightening his arms, working his fingers, and rubbing his back, which itched constantly. As part of his therapy and to strengthen him—and to get us out of the house!—I would walk with Brian around our local mall.

For his wound care, every evening after supper, I removed his bandages and took him downstairs to our large, double-sized shower. We used the downstairs shower because the stall was large enough for both of us. Since he was unable to bathe himself, he would sit on a chair while I would hold a washcloth above his wounds and squeeze the soapy water onto those areas. Then I would rinse.

After the shower I patted him dry, wrapped him tightly in blankets, and helped him back upstairs, walking on the gravity side in case he fell. He was still very wobbly on stairs and would be unable to catch himself.

I would start his treatment by putting Mercurochrome on his open wounds to try to get those to close. Then it was scar massage: I rubbed all the scars to try to break up and loosen the scar tissue to smooth out the skin. After that, I put all the different lotions, creams, and medications on him to keep infections away, help with the healing process, and soothe the pain.

Next I helped him put on his pajamas and put him into his bed. When he was settled, I gave him his medication for the night. That was our nightly routine. The entire process after supper took two hours.

★ *Brian*

I wore tight compression garments on my hands and arms twenty-three hours a day. They were thick pressure gloves that went all the way up my arms and felt like thermal underwear, three sizes too small. The garments were incredibly uncomfortable and painful because they felt as if they were cutting off my circulation. I also wore a black headband on my forehead. The garments helped to reduce scarring or bumps, called *keloids,* and to keep flat what scarring was already there. The skin grafts produce bumps; the garments flatten them. They kept a tight fit over my arms so that as my skin contracted they provided constant pressure to keep the skin flat and smooth. Otherwise the skin would become rough, tumbled, and scab-pocked. I was to wear those compression garments for thirteen months.

The only time those garments came off was when I showered. Because the new skin was like baby skin and the garments caused friction, the friction caused blisters.

After my shower Mel had to pop each blister with a needle, drain the water from it, then put Mercurochrome on it to dry it out. Once the blisters were dry and the scar massage was done, the garments went back on. It always felt like a wrestling match because they were so tight. Mel would place pantyhose on my arms before she put on the gloves and pressure garments. The pantyhose made it a little easier to slide the garments.

Dr. Jordan informed us that because of the extent of my burns, my skin would continue to scar and contract for more than a year. That meant more surgeries.

★ *Mel*

My life was consumed with caring for Brian and giving attention to Matt. Except for the hour in the morning when I read my Bible and prayed, I didn't have one moment to myself.

The instant I sat down, I would hear, "Mel, I need . . ." or "Mom, I need . . ."

I was nurse, wife, mother, maid, chef, chauffeur, physical therapist, counselor, advisor, scheduler, secretary, bill payer, and nag. Being a nag was the easiest part. Brian says I dragged him through this experience. I say I nagged him through it.

All the different responsibilities became too much at times, and I would have meltdowns. I would go to my room, close the door, and cry.

★ *Brian*

Mel tried to hide it when she was upset or overwhelmed. She never wanted me to see her cry. But I knew how difficult this was for her.

Everything was piled on her. She became a single parent to two children—one of whom needed constant care! It pained me every time I needed to ask her for assistance. I desperately wanted life to go back to pre-September 11 when I was a vital part of our household. Many times I felt more like a burden than an asset.

Although I knew I should not think that way, sometimes it was hard not to. I realized what a gift I had in Mel. She understood what marriage was about. It was about sticking through the tough times. There was nothing she didn't do for me, no bodily fluid she hadn't dealt with. She'd seen and done it all—and yet she was still committed to me. That made me love her even more—even though I failed to express that well in such a time of pain. I hoped I would never have to care for her the way she'd cared for me. Yet if I had to, I hoped I could do as well for her as she did for me.

One day soon after Christmas, I stepped from the shower and noticed a small hole, like a bullet hole, in my skin just above my left elbow. The scars were contracting and pulling my skin apart. It left a hole that was oozing pus.

We panicked. With every move the hole seemed to widen. It looked as if it was infected and torn all the way down to the muscle.

Mel called the burn center, crying and upset. The nurse said, "That's fine. It's normal. There's nothing to worry about." The nurse explained that we wanted the skin to stretch and that holes were okay because they were helping the skin stretch. The challenge was to keep them free from infection. The nurse advised Mel to place a large amount of Bactriban, an antibiotic cream, in the hole and the next time Brian was at the hospital they would evaluate it.

On January 2, 2002, I returned to the hospital for surgery on that elbow. Dr. Jordan made two incisions, two upside down Vs, on each side of the tearing elbow to release the contracture and take care of the ripping.

Dr. Jordan also worked on the webbing for my left hand. I had lost the webbing between my index finger and thumb in the fire, which left my hand acting similar to a lobster claw. Dr. Jordan reconstructed my thumb. He inserted a screw through my thumb bone, through my hand,

and into the index finger bone. The screw would ensure that the thumb wouldn't contract back toward the hand again. Dr. Jordan covered it with more grafting, wrapped it with Xeriform (the yellow, moist mineral oil wrapping), and covered that with a huge ball of cotton.

Dr. Jordan placed a piece of cork over the end of the screw that protruded from the cotton so I wouldn't hurt myself if I bumped it.

Because we were returning home in a few days, Dr. Jordan wanted Mel to do the dressing change so she could become used to working with the new skin grafts.

The grafts are so delicate that the least little thing can cause my body to reject it. The first attempt to change the bandage proved disastrous. As Mel lifted the bandage, the graft started to come off. Her eyes widened, then filled with tears.

"I have totally undone everything they've done!" she cried.

Dr. Jordan said, "That's okay, Mel." He handed her a pair of tweezers and instructed her to gently lay the graft back into place and cover it with more Xeriform.

The next surgery was scheduled for February to relieve the contractures on the other elbow. While the surgery helped tremendously, it didn't completely correct the problem; my elbow had grown excess bone that kept the joint from moving freely.

Life was definitely different. But I was alive—and I was home.

SIXTEEN
The Media

JOURNAL 11/14/01
Brian just finished his surgery. Right eye, left arm this time. Nightline
filmed the surgery.

★*Mel*

From the moment I checked our answering machine the night of September 11, the media inundated us with interview requests. Hundreds of newspaper and television reporters wanted to speak with us, including international people. The most surprising request came from Al Jazeera, the Arabic television network that ran stories of the celebrations some people in the Arabic world held on 9/11. (We turned down that request.)

Somehow the media discovered the survivors' names. Because our phone number was listed, reporters did easy research and began calling our home phone number.

We wanted as little to do with the media as possible, so initially I ignored or said no to all media requests. I felt that since this was Brian's story, he needed to make the decisions over which interviews to grant. As Brian became more conscious, I told him, "We have all this media we need to respond to."

He told me flatly, "Don't talk to anybody but Fox News or Rush Limbaugh." By that point the story about the President's visit and Brian's attempted salute had been reported on Rush Limbaugh's radio show and Web site. That story was the first media report about Brian that was released. Colonel Rota, who was in Brian's room during the President's visit, returned to the Pentagon that day and told everybody in his department about the moment. Rich Galen, a conservative commentator who publishes an online newsletter called *Mullings,* discovered the story and posted it on his Web site. Rush Limbaugh read the story and mentioned the salute on his show, wondering if it was a true story. Brian's brother, Wade, who was listening to the radio show that day, e-mailed Rush and said, "I'm Lieutenant Colonel Brian Birdwell's big brother. Yes, it's a true story."

Wade called me immediately to tell me about it. I found a radio and took it into Brian's room and told Brian the news. Brian loves Rush and listens to him all the time. But Brian's response to me was, "So what?" He was in so much pain he didn't care about anything other than alleviating the hurt. It was just too overwhelming for him to try to listen to anything other than music.

Toward the end of September, Paul and Holly Fine, producers of ABC's *Nightline,* gathered all the families and proposed doing a special story on how a Burn Unit operates. They guaranteed it would not be focused on our families or individuals. Everyone declined.

About a month later Paul and Holly returned a second time and approached Mike Kurtz and me. They said, "We'd really like to focus on Brian and Louise."

I talked to Brian about it, and we decided to pray before we made our decision. We felt our appearance on *Nightline* could be a way for us to tell a national audience what God had done in our lives.

I told Paul that Brian and I had been discussing his proposal and we were interested, under one condition—that we could openly and freely discuss our faith in God.

"The rule in television," Paul told me, "is that God is left on the cutting-room floor. You don't air that stuff. However, your faith is so integral to your story that if we put God on the cutting-room floor, we would have no story. I give you my word that your faith will remain in this story."

We said yes.

When we agreed to do *Nightline,* we really thought that would be the end of the media coverage on us. But it turned into much more than that.

Brian did end up on Fox News Network, his favorite. But he also made appearances on *The Oprah Winfrey Show*, *Nightline*, CBN, CNN, MSNBC, and local television stations. And he was interviewed for *U.S. News & World Report* and *The Washington Post*.

Every major news station or newspaper contacted us. People responded en masse to the Kansas City sportswriter, who wrote an article about Brian and what a huge Chiefs fan he was, then suggested that people send Brian a card. Each day we received three to five tubs of letters and packages from Chiefs fans. Sometimes it took me two trips to carry all the mail from Brian's room to the hotel.

I read the letters while Brian was in surgery or having his dressings changed. Each letter was encouraging. People we didn't know sent their support. It was incredible to open these letters and feel the outpouring of love from total strangers.

At the same time, though, it became an impossible task to try to respond to each letter. While I did my best, I know I failed miserably.

★*Mel*

The requests for interviews continued to flood in. Thank God for Karen Baker and Elaine Kanellis in Army Public Affairs. They volunteered to take care of the requests and to deal with the media for us. When we received a call, we would respond, "You have to call Army Public Affairs. We can't make the decision about doing an interview because Brian is an active duty officer." It felt wonderful to pass that off.

Of all the media, Paul and Holly Fine, who produced *Nightline*, were the most sensitive to our situation. They followed us daily while we were in the hospital, filming everything including physical therapy sessions and surgeries. They captured our good moments and the times when we were hurting. *Nightline* ran an hour show on the six-month anniversary of the attack, then another hour show on the one-year anniversary.

The day Brian was discharged and we moved from the Burn Unit to the hotel, the Fines took our family to Morton's Steakhouse to film us returning to normal life. They filmed normal life all right! Taking Matt to a fancy restaurant is always an experience. Morton's Steakhouse has the distinction of allowing you to choose the exact cut of steak you want. The waiter pushed out the cart filled with meat selections, and as Matt reached across the cart to point to his choice, a lobster that was just below Matt's arm seemed to come alive and began to move his claw toward Matt. Matt, of course, screamed—and everybody laughed. We had a wonderful time; it took our minds off everything that had happened to us.

★ *Brian*

As the reality of our story becoming a national story began to sink in, we were dumbstruck. *Why would they want to talk to us?* we often wondered. *We're just normal people. Boring, average people! There's nothing special or spectacular about us.*

Yet we discovered that God was using us through opportunities in the media. He provided a public platform to allow us to tell what he did in our lives. For whatever reason, God chose to use us. I felt it was an honor to have been chosen by God.

People began to refer to me as a celebrity. I cringed every time I heard someone use that word. I was still just Brian.

My first live interview was on the Fox News Network. I was sitting in the studio awaiting word from the producer that they were ready for me to go on the air, when Brit Hume and another man entered. Mr. Hume introduced himself, then said, "This is my pastor. We'd like to pray with you, if that's okay."

"Absolutely!" I said. "That would be an honor."

Mr. Hume was aware of my story and my interest in making sure my faith was an integral part of every interview. So his pastor prayed that my words would glorify God.

The media attention opened opportunities for us to speak publicly. The first place I was invited to speak was at the Pentagon prayer breakfast in February 2002. Chaplain Haynes, the Pentagon chaplain, called me at home and offered the invitation. I accepted.

I promptly hung up the phone and prayed, *Okay, Lord, what is it we need to say?* That's when Mel and I sat down and discussed what we had learned through our experiences. We talked about God's grace and the miracles that had happened in our lives. We realized that while our situation is extreme and interesting because of the 9/11 angle, there were still a lot of areas from our story that would be relevant to other people. At some point everybody is going to experience pain, whether it's physical, emotional, or spiritual. We wanted to tell people, "We know what you're going through. We've been there. There's hope and healing available to you."

Not everyone would experience the extreme survival situation that Mel and I had to face. However, everyone at some point will face a trial or challenge in life that will compel them to desperately call for God's mercy and peace. We don't always know why God allows things to happen. But we are confident from our experience that he is always with us, carrying us through—whether it's the physical challenges I'm facing or the emotional challenges Mel confronts as she watches me experience my pain.

The most important spiritual concept we learned was about experiencing the peace only Christ can bring. In those seconds inside the Pentagon when I was on fire, going from the struggle to survive to acknowledging the reality of my death, I went from panic to calm. Who else can provide that except Christ?

Mel and I decided that we needed to share the reality of God's sovereignty—especially in the midst of hardships. After having gone through something as horrific as what Mel and Matt and I experienced, we knew how important depending on God's sovereignty was.

The morning of the prayer breakfast Mel and I walked in and wondered if we were in the right place. I used to attend that breakfast every Wednesday morning in the Pentagon before 9/11. There would be maybe thirty or forty people.

The morning I was to speak, however, the prayer breakfast was booked for the entire executive dining room—and it was packed. There were about two hundred people there, including Secretary White and other VIPs. I looked at Mel and said, "Did they get the right guy for this? Maybe we're at a different prayer breakfast." We couldn't believe the attendance. We also wondered if this was a foretelling of what was about to come our way regarding invitations to speak.

I think the most profound thing for Mel and me has been sharing Jesus Christ with people. People look at us and say, "If you got through the horrific things you had to deal with, what am I complaining about with the challenge I face?"

While Mel and I never sought the media attention that came our way, we tried to accept most of the media invitations so that the great message about faith in God could be made public. We've taken the commission to share Christ boldly, and that's what we've tried to do. We didn't accept the media spotlight because it would draw attention to us. It has simply been to give God the credit for bringing us through the fire. There have been those interviews that have edited out God, and there have been those that haven't. We don't have control over the interviews or what is printed or aired. But we've tried to be faithful in our mission to speak for the *Lord's* glory, not ours.

SEVENTEEN

Learning through the Pain

JOURNAL 10/26/01

Thank you for your truths. When I grasp the truth that all things are working together for good to conform me to God's image, then what am I to do in ALL my circumstances? According to 1 Thessalonians 5:18: "In everything give thanks; for this is God's will for you in Christ Jesus." Lord, I want to give thanks in all things.

★*Brian*

I've been to hell and back. Alone, in intense agony, and afraid was how I imagined hell to be. The events inside the Pentagon, going from light to dark and enduring the fire that was consuming me, will forever remain with me.

The pain was not only physical; it was emotional and spiritual. Before the explosion I was in a building that was very familiar to me. After the explosion I lost my sense of direction. Complete panic gripped my mind. There were no lights to help me see. I had no ability to breathe and no ability to navigate. I had no idea of the way to safety—or the way to danger.

As I was lying on the floor waiting to die, I thought of Mel and Matt and the good-byes we'd shared that morning. I truly believed that was the last time I would see them. I wondered how they would deal with my death and thought of the reality that we would not meet again until eternity.

How well I've learned that life is fragile. We do not know when death will come. For me, it could have been in only fifteen seconds. Fifteen seconds of lying in a blazing building, a building about to collapse. In those few short moments, the reality of eternity, the reality of hell crashed down on me.

The amazing thing was that even while I was in the midst of burning,

God was working to meet my needs. The Lord has a miraculous way of fixing our problems. Shortly after I collapsed to the floor and gave up, convinced I was going to die, suffocating under the weight of three pains—physical, emotional, and spiritual—God was working on my behalf. I went from being on fire to being extinguished. I went from being unable to navigate to being able to move on down the corridor. I went from thinking I was dying to knowing I could survive. In those same minutes of chaos, panic, and terror, the Lord put those things at rest in my heart.

★*Mel*

Brian's pain was the physical pain. He endured more than I can ever imagine. Yet he rarely complained.

Brian didn't discuss in-depth the events of 9/11 with me until a month later when he was in step-down care. Out of the blue Brian began talking about the escape and told me that when he collapsed in the corridor at the Pentagon, he landed under a sprinkler, which extinguished the fire. I was so deeply thankful to God for saving Brian's life. Brian's story was another reminder that God walked through this ordeal with us. He didn't leave us to deal with this alone.

Yet I still struggled. My pain was the emotional pain of not knowing the future. I cannot describe adequately my feelings of sitting on my couch, watching the burning building I knew my husband was in, and not knowing whether he was alive or dead. Then spending days in ICU, not knowing if he would be alive from moment to moment.

Watching him endure such intense pain was often unbearable for me. I wanted to fix it, to take it away. I couldn't; I was helpless. I could only pray and be there for him.

One of the most devastating aspects of pain is the utter fear that grips and paralyzes you. I became paranoid and irrational. I struggled with severe panic attacks. My heart would race, and I would have difficulty breathing. Fear totally encapsulated me, and I was overcome with a sense of urgency that something horrible was about to happen.

Any time I traveled, anxiety would overtake me. I was afraid I would be involved in an accident that would leave my son without either parent to care for him. I prayed continually for safe travel and protection. I worried over the anthrax scare. I worried that Brian would die or that the hospital staff would make a mistake in his care. I would often ask God, *Why do I allow fear to reign in me? Don't let fear control my mind.*

I felt weak and powerless. I was frightened to leave Brian, even though I knew he was ultimately in God's hands. Every day I had to give up my need for control and trust that God would work in Brian's life.

I could only pray and tell myself that this fear was not rational and nothing bad was going to happen. There was nothing else I could do.

I would find Scripture verses that specifically talked about fear. Psalm 23:4 says, "Even though I walk through the valley of the shadow of death, I fear no evil, for You are with me." There were so many Scriptures in which God continually said, "Fear not." I tried to focus my mind on those passages—that God was with me, so I had nothing to fear.

It became a matter of praying for patience and endurance and for renewed strength, minute by minute, day by day, to be able to get through whatever that day and that night and the next day held, because I never knew what was waiting around the corner.

★ *Brian*

Taking care of burns is as much a psychological care as it is physiological. I was mentally anguished because I was completely dependent on other people—to bathe me, feed me, help me use the restroom. There was *nothing* I could do on my own. I even needed a ventilator to help me breathe.

Understanding my distress, Mel would pray with me every morning and ask God to give me a good day. I kept trying to look at my struggles and progress in the light of eternity. I would think, *Yes, this may be two or three years of suffering, but in Christ's view it's just a nanosecond of eternity. So I can get through this.*

It was difficult to maintain that perspective. I could *know* it, but it was often difficult to *live* it. When I was able to live it, the suffering became tolerable.

★ *Mel*

One of the most difficult things for me in going through our "fire" was dealing with uncompassionate, uncaring, or just unknowing people. I struggled with how I was to be a strong advocate for Brian and still honor God in my treatment of arduous people. Initially I coped with it by telling them, "My only priority right now is my husband, who is fighting for his life." While I prayed continually about my responses, many times I snapped.

At times I would plead with God to give me the ability to close my mouth and not to say something that would be hurtful or cause bigger implications later. I prayed that somehow through this experience I would glorify God. But I had to revisit that issue with God over and over.

One instance occurred when I contacted Brian's cell phone company because his phone was destroyed at the Pentagon. I explained the situation to the customer service person and said, "I need to know what to do to get his phone replaced." The rep told me, "It's going to cost you six hundred dollars."

"Do you understand that terrorists flew a plane into the building and that the phone burned?"

"Yes, ma'am, but your contract says you are obligated to pay for replacing a lost phone."

There were so many stumbling blocks. They were little speed bumps, but they felt like mountains in front of me at the time. So I prayed, asking for a lot of forgiveness. At times I was successful in keeping quiet and other times I failed.

Matthew struggled too. He told me he would sit with his friends after homeschool and think, *Is my dad going to live or die?* He would see his friends with their parents and would think about how much he missed us and how alone he felt. He tried to be brave.

It was very important to both Brian and me that Matt understood that God was taking care of Brian. There was nothing evil people could do to his dad that we couldn't overcome. I prayed that even though I couldn't be there around the clock for Matt that he would know he could still lean on God. I prayed that his faith in God would be strengthened, especially when Debbie Vance told me about their evening prayer times. At night when they prayed with the boys, they would all take turns praying—everyone, that is, except Matt. He would never pray out loud; he would only sit quietly and stare. That wasn't like Matt. Matt would always pray out loud at our house. I desperately wanted this experience to end for him. I wanted our home and our life to be normal. There were so many changes that Matt had to cope with, so much upheaval that wasn't fair. I would think about that, and the guilt would grow again.

Yet even in the midst of all the guilt and pain, I never wanted to quit, never wanted to walk away. I wanted the *situation* to go away. I wanted a day in which I didn't have to deal with the stress or pressure or anxiety or worries. Mostly my only reprieve was to escape to my hotel room, where I would go to pray or cry.

There was never a moment when I was afraid that if Brian survived he would be a shell of the person he once was or that our relationship would change so much I would not know him anymore. There were times when Brian would ask me, "Am I going to be able to do things I did before?" I would tell him I didn't know. I tried not to dwell on those things because I knew that no matter what the future held, nothing could be worse than experiencing 9/11.

There were so many things that helped me survive: I said a lot of prayers and wrote in my journal because I couldn't tell anybody else all the things I was thinking and feeling.

Any time of the day or night I could call my friend Karen Mann and cry, and she would pray with me and reassure me. She's one of the few people who told me from the beginning that God had given her a peace about Brian, that he was going to heal. I clung to that.

The families of the other burn survivors were also a tremendous encouragement. We formed a tight group and depended on one another. We took turns having our meltdowns and comforting each other. We became and still are very close. We were each others' support group.

Knowing that Brian needed me so much was a comfort. At least I was making some contribution to his recovery, even if it was just being there. It was after he came home and was totally dependent on me that I felt the situation became too much to handle at times.

Probably the first realization of how tough it was going to be was the first night he was out of the hospital. I was afraid to sleep in the same bed with him because I was worried I would scratch or bump him during the night. He wanted to lie on his stomach because he hadn't done that since September 10. He wiggled himself around—but his arms were still at almost ninety-degree angles. He lay in that position for a few seconds and began screaming in pain because he was stretching muscles that hadn't been stretched. I physically picked him up and flipped him over without touching his arms.

I lifted and moved him a lot of times during those first weeks he was home, and moving him was like moving dead weight! Because I knew he was completely my responsibility, I did things I thought I never could do.

As a caregiver every second of my day was taken up with meeting someone else's needs. I couldn't take time to care for myself. And I was worn out. Basically, I was ready to crash.

And I did. After a period of months, I got to the point where if I heard Brian say my name one more time or tell me that he needed something, I felt as though I would scream. I didn't want to be the caregiver anymore. I would become frustrated and angry and resentful—and then catch myself and feel guilty, because I knew that wasn't who I really was. I wanted to be a loving, good, kind, and gentle spouse. I just didn't have anything left to give.

★ Brian

As I look back over our ordeal, I realize there were three things that brought me through: my faith in God, a supportive spouse, and a sense of humor.

I cannot imagine going through this experience without faith. My faith allowed me not only to heal physically but to heal spiritually and emotionally. Some unbelievers may call it having a good attitude. Others may call it good karma. But I know it was the sovereign hand of God and my relationship with the Creator that brought me through this ordeal.

I was blessed to have a supportive spouse—even during her struggles. I was a forty-year-old baby lying in that bed, and Mel stayed with me. I had her encouragement, always knowing that she loved me absolutely and would be my advocate, my protector. But to share our faith, to have her pray with me was the most important. Having Mel read Scripture to me many times felt far better than having the nurse sit with me checking instruments or heart rates.

We also learned to laugh together. Unarguably, what happened to us was horrific. However, being able to laugh did more to keep going. The Bible says in Proverbs 17:22: "A joyful heart is good medicine, but a broken spirit dries up the bones."

We laugh about my being a crispy old man. And every time we drive by a Kentucky Fried Chicken, we always laugh because the colonel's original recipe and extra crispy have a whole new meaning! I joke that I'm 40 percent original recipe, 60 percent extra crispy. While that kind of thing is funny to think about, when you're sitting in your home alone, your sense of humor is not what is going to help you cope with the gravity of your experience and your future.

A sense of humor is a reflection of understanding God's grace and sovereignty in my life and in the problems we faced. That grace is what allows me the opportunity to laugh about looking the way I do and laugh about not being able to do certain things. The Lord has been gracious enough to grant me life, and there are things we can laugh about because God has handled the serious things.

I can look at old photos of myself before the attack and say, "Wow, I had huge ears." There are also times I say, "I wish I had ears. I wish I wasn't scarred." Those scars are not pleasant. But they are a daily reminder of God's grace in my life. They help me appreciate what it means to be alive.

While those who don't acknowledge God's sovereignty in their lives may physically heal, a sense of humor will bring them no solace. They don't have the hope of eternal salvation. Their hope is in themselves and what this earth has to offer.

A sense of humor taught us how to learn what's important and what isn't. Those things that aren't important, such as looks, we've learned to take lightly.

★*Mel*

The book of Romans spoke to me about suffering. In Romans 5:2-5 the apostle Paul reminds us,

We exult in hope of the glory of God. And not only this, but we also exult in our tribulations, knowing that tribulation brings about perseverance; and perseverance, proven character; and proven character, hope; and hope does not disappoint, because the love of God has been poured out within our hearts through the Holy Spirit who was given to us.

And Paul says also in Romans 8:18, "I consider that the sufferings of this present time are not worthy to be compared with the glory that is to be revealed to us." When I read those passages, they remind me of all the suffering Brian has been through.

I believe one of the reasons God allows us to suffer to the extent we do is so that we will be drawn closer to him. Because through everything we've endured, God was our solid Rock; we clung to him passionately. We could not have gone through this nightmare without the strength of the Lord. Nothing I could ever have done myself would have gotten me through that.

★ Brian

I found comfort in knowing that Christ had also suffered. He is our suffering Savior. I could ask for his comfort when I prayed, "Okay, Lord, you've been through this. You know the physical aspects of what we're feeling. Grant us comfort." Jesus experienced far worse than I did, so how could I complain? I had a medical staff and a wonderful wife taking care of me. I had no reason to snivel. Putting that in perspective sustained me through many painful times.

★ Mel

When Brian was first out of the hospital, I would wake up each morning and gaze at him. Then I'd touch him to make sure he was still there. To me, he's a living miracle. In those early days at home I was thankful to be able to do that; I still am.

When we look back on how far Brian has come, we celebrate. God has indeed proven himself faithful. He has turned our mourning into joy (Jeremiah 31:13).

EIGHTEEN

Going Back

JOURNAL 10/31/01
Lord, lead us to the place where he will do the best in terms of returning to normal.

★*Brian*

On March 12, 2002, six months after 9/11, I had enough strength to return to work part-time.

For the first month I worked for a few hours every Tuesday and Thursday and did physical therapy the other days. Then we'd switch to Mondays, Wednesdays, and Fridays, with PT on the switched days, until late June when I returned to full-time status.

On the first day I returned to work, Mel woke me at 5:15 that morning. She helped me dress because I was still unable to put on my shirt or tuck it in. She buttoned the top button of my uniform, tied my tie, and helped me with my jacket. I was Mel's life-sized Ken doll!

I wanted everything to be perfect, so I was a bit edgy with Mel. Not because I wanted her to dress me properly. It was more the anticipation of realizing, *I'm going back to work!*

She grabbed my computer bag, checked the compression garments on my hands and forehead, and helped me into our car.

As we pulled up to the Pentagon, I noticed the construction crews were hard at work. The plan was to have the damaged section rebuilt by September 11, 2002, one year after the attack. They were six months from completion and working around the clock. There was little left to indicate there had been a terrorist attack. No ghastly gash—just soot marks along the top of the building's west side.

★*Mel*

It was a strange day for me because a *Nightline* crew came to our house at five in the morning to video Brian's entire first day back to work. They arrived before we were out of bed! I was awakened that morning to the sound of the doorbell ringing and to banging on our front door.

I hadn't slept well the night before because I was worried about Brian going back to work. He had depended on me for the last six months. Now he was becoming independent again. I was concerned that he would become overly tired or frustrated if he couldn't do something on his own.

While that morning was difficult for me, I was happy for Brian because he was *so* excited to be going back to work. He is a soldier to his core. He kept saying, "It's great to be a soldier again!"

General Keane, Vice Chief of Staff of the Army, had visited Brian in the hospital and assured him a place in the Army. And Major General Van Antwerp had assured him that there would always be a place for him in ACSIM. Brian needed to hear his superiors say those words. It gave him a goal to aim for: He *had* to get better so he could return to work.

As I drove him to the Pentagon there was a huge hollow ache in my stomach. I parked in the parking lot by Corridor 2 and walked him to the edge of the building, where I took a few photos and hugged him.

"I'm so proud of you," I whispered to him and then left him to go about his day. Leaving him there felt like the first day I'd dropped off Matt at kindergarten. *Will they take care of him?* I wondered. I walked back to my car, got in, and cried the whole way home.

★*Brian*

Going back that first day was incredible. It was a great day simply because it was a "win" for me. A lot of people asked me if I was able to handle going back into the building because of the memories. I never experienced any nervousness or anxiety about returning. I *needed* to go back. Stepping back into the place that could have—that *should* have— been my murder scene was important to me. I stepped back a winner. I was a walking miracle, a testimony to what God did for me that day. We were winning; the terrorists weren't. I was going back to work; I was returning to normalcy.

For me, there is holy ground inside the Pentagon. That place is where the Lord conducted one of his greatest miracles. It's ground to be honored, not to be feared. And so not to return to work would be to admit defeat.

There were three of us in my office on September 11. Two were killed. If I didn't return, then we would be batting 0 for 3. I don't know why the Lord chose me to be the one of the three who lived, but one of us was *going* to go back.

I wasn't going back into that building to remember the bad that came from the building. I was going back to remember the good that came out of it. It was my way of defiantly saying, "I didn't just survive on my own. My God helped me survive. I'm still here. You want a piece of me? Give it another try."

★ *Mel*

Brian was completely surrounded by an entourage of people with cameras and microphones. Paul and Holly Fine from *Nightline* were there with their camera crew, plus all the local affiliates that were filming Brian's every move.

I was glad the cameras were with Brian. Since they were filming him I could see what he was doing! While I realized I could have gone with him and spent the day at the Pentagon, I knew he needed to do this alone. It was his day, and I didn't want to be in the way. Later I was able to watch what happened even though I wasn't there. That was a nice reward.

★ *Brian*

Just walking through the Pentagon was a workout. It was a long walk! I was huffing and puffing, thinking, *I don't remember it being this long.* I had to stop at one of the snack bars to sit and rest. Everybody kept asking, "Are you okay? You want me to carry your bags?"

"I'm fine," I told them. "And no, I'll carry my bags. I have to do this on my own."

I started walking again and saw Dave Davis, a contractor for the Army and our Sunday school president, in the hallway. While he knew I was out of the hospital, he had no idea I was returning to work. I was glad to see a familiar face, so I stopped and said hi. As we spoke I saw tears form in his eyes.

The ACSIM headquarters, which had moved back to its pre-9/11 office space, was filled with "welcome back" banners and balloons. I was completely surprised! Everyone was smiling and seemed genuinely happy to see me. It was great.

My duty before 9/11 was as the military aide for Ms. Jan Menig, deputy ACSIM. After my previous coworkers greeted me, Ms. Menig arrived. She warmly welcomed me with a big hug and then walked me to another department—the ACSIM resource division. My assignment in the Pentagon was changed because I would no longer be able to handle the intense tasks I used to, such as working sixteen-hour-days to keep track of Ms. Menig's schedule.

My new coworkers were waiting to welcome me when we arrived in the resource division. My nameplate had even been placed on my new cubicle. And my new boss? Colonel Dane Rota. That's right—Mel's right-hand man while I was in the hospital. This was yet another "God thing."

I stayed only for a few hours my first day because my endurance still wasn't built up. I was easily exhausted.

On that first day back I didn't return to the area that had been destroyed. It was still under construction. But several months later I walked down Corridor 4, the site where my life changed forever.

As I started down the corridor, Colonel Roy Wallace, who had rescued me on 9/11, stepped into the hallway. He was shocked when he saw me.

"Looks a lot different from the last time we met here," he said.

"Sure does," I answered. "It's holy ground down there."

I wanted to piece together exactly what had happened, and I wanted to see where I had been standing in relation to the plane's point of impact. The plane came in between Corridors 4 and 5. It penetrated very closely to where Corridor 4 makes a T with the E-Ring. I was to the right of the plane as it penetrated the building on a perpendicular angle. As I marked the spot where I had been versus where the plane entered the building, I shuddered.

Fifteen to twenty yards from the point of impact. *That's two car-lengths*, I thought. *I* really *should not be alive*. There's no rational, logical reason for me to be alive, except that the hand of God protected me.

God can use a trip to the restroom for his glory! Had I remained in the office, I would have died. (I sat four windows from the point of impact.) Had I left my office any sooner, I would have been in the path of the plane. Had I left any later, I would have been in the path of the plane.

After leaving the men's room, I had turned right and made it to the first set of elevators when the plane struck. I was actually hit from two sides. The flames rushed the short distance around the corner to where I was, but the worst blast came from the overpressurization in the elevators. The fire probably traveled through the elevator shaft and blasted open and through the doors. I think that's where the *whoosh* sound came from. It happened so quickly I didn't have a chance to react.

In a fire an elevator shaft acts like a vacuum, and fires follow the path of least resistance. The fire will be channeled through the length of the elevator shaft. I think that's how the roof of the Pentagon caught on fire. Part of the fourth corridor was burned on the roof all the way down to the A-ring. It's like driving a car on the expressway with no other traffic. You can fly unhindered. So the elevator shaft becomes an expressway in a fire; it can travel unhindered from all the floors. That's why they tell you not to get on elevators in a fire.

There was a lady in New York, Lauren Manning, who was burned severely in the World Trade Center. She spent a lot of time at a burn unit in New York. What was surprising about her story was that she was on the ground floor when the building was hit—more than seventy floors from the penetration point. When the plane exploded in the building, the blast rushed through the elevator shafts. It was channelized and blew open the elevator doors in the lobby. She happened to be standing in front of one of the elevators and was burned.

Just after Christmas a professional engineer, Georgina, was doing an analysis of the Pentagon so they could improve the structure as they rebuilt it. She visited a few of the survivors to discuss their stories with them and find out what they did to survive. She showed me the diagram of where all the people had died. Sandi was still standing, watching the television when the plane came through. She didn't have a chance. She died immediately. Cheryle had stepped back into the main office area. Had Jan Menig been in her office, she, too, would have died instantly.

The recovery scenes were incredibly gruesome, depicting what a ghastly death this was. Everything had happened so quickly.

I don't consider myself a victim. I am a survivor. Yes, I have been victimized because I was the victim of other people's evil decisions. I didn't choose to go through this experience of my own volition. But to me, the real victims are the ones who died that day. I still have my life; they do not.

★ *Mel*

After that first day I visited Brian at the Pentagon frequently. As the year anniversary approached, Brian would say to me, "Let's go down to Corridor 4 so you can see where I was standing." We would start down the corridor, but as soon as we reached the C-Ring, I would stop walking. I just could go no farther. There were signs posted everywhere that said, *Hard Hats. Construction Area. Do Not Enter.*

I would use those signs as my excuse. "Brian, it says, 'Hard Hats.' We can't go in there."

He would say, "No, we can go down this side. It's fine."

But I was adamant. "No, I don't want to go." I wasn't ready to see the spot. Even though the debris and wreckage were removed and there were no traces of the attack, I wasn't ready to see the crime scene.

He took me down that corridor on several occasions. And every time the same thing would happen. I couldn't go all the way to stand in the spot where Brian could have died.

Finally, on September 11, 2002, the wedge was completely opened. I had no more excuses. We walked slowly down the corridor, and once we were at the end of the hall, we stopped. Brian said, "This is where I was standing."

I could visualize everything clearly: the elevator door, the metal seams where the building collapsed, the walls and offices where the plane came into the building. I saw how extremely close he had been to the point of impact. I saw the distance of the plane to his office.

That's when I knew how right Brian was. I was indeed standing on holy ground. The realization became overwhelming to me, and I felt a strong urge just to kneel on the floor and cry out to God, thanking him for his blessing. Here stood my husband who should not have been alive—yet he was alive.

My emotions started to take over. I began to feel weak in my knees, and my stomach felt queasy. By God's grace a friend of ours turned the corner, saw us, and walked toward us. That was the distraction I needed to regain control of my emotions.

★ Brian

On September 11, 2002, one year after the horrific attack, the damaged wedge of the building was reopened. On the first floor there is a chapel with a permanent memorial to remember all the innocent men, women, and children who died in the attack on the Pentagon: 184, not counting the terrorists. More people died here than in the Oklahoma City bombing. The windows of the memorial are covered with the Kevlar-coating, a yellow-green substance to make sure the windows are blast-proof.

As I walked into the memorial room, I noticed that the tinted windows provided an eerie quiet. I looked at the wall that listed the names. My eyes scanned the list. There were the names I knew would be recorded but wished weren't: Cheryle Sincock and Sandi Taylor. I felt that anguish in my soul again over their loss. It was an empty, hollow ache, a desperate longing to see them again. In my heart I promised them that their lives would not have been lost in vain. I would survive to tell the story.

NINETEEN
Reaching Out

JOURNAL 10/27/01
Paul, Brian's night nurse, came in to give Brian his pain meds and taught me how to take off these bandages. Paul began asking Brian about 9/11. Brian, who'd had a wretched day and had no plug on his trachea tube, in a very strong voice began to share the gospel with Paul. He explained how God had spared his life by providing sprinklers, rescuers, and medical attention to allow him to be able to share his story and God's glory. It was an awesome moment. You could feel the presence of the Lord in the room.

★ *Brian*

Mel and I were always okay about talking about our faith. But we never did it blatantly. It was usually just a personal thing that we would share if we knew someone else was a Christian or if someone had a question. Mostly we lived out our faith quietly. I didn't share very often with co-workers. I'd go to the Wednesday morning devotionals or else had my own. I always had a devotional book and a Bible on my desk. But we weren't outspoken in our faith.

September 11 changed all of that.

I felt what I can only imagine hell will feel like. That was enough for me to want to try to warn everybody. I became much more forthright about my relationship with Jesus. Not that I walk up to people today, shake them, and yell, "Do you know the Lord?!" But I no longer allow opportunities to pass by without saying something. It's no longer about being a quiet witness in which I simply expect my life to lead someone to Christ without ever uttering a word. The events of 9/11 afford me the opportunity in a short period of time to share a bit about God's grace in our lives, hopefully leaving that question in someone's mind: *If that's the*

kind of attitude this guy can have after what happened to him, there's got to
be something to this Christian thing.

One day Mel read Jude 1:23 to me: "Save others, snatching them out of the fire." I started to think about that verse's meaning. I was saved from a literal, physical fire. But Jude talks about the spiritual fire of hell. He was saying that as we go out and tell the good news about Jesus Christ, we will snatch some people out of eternal damnation, the fire of hell.

That's when I realized the importance of what I was going through. I knew what the fire felt like. And I wanted to do everything I could to make sure no one had to experience that for eternity. If going through this experience and being able to relay that information to people allows one person to start a relationship with God, then what happened to me has not been in vain. That may have been God's whole purpose. Maybe God kept me alive to bring a passion and a fervor to my words. When I say, "You need to get right with God *now* because you don't know when you're going to die," I know of what I speak.

Our experience has made talking about Jesus much easier. How God saved me tells it all! There is no one who can approach us and scoff after we show them the photo of where I was and talk to them about the injuries I sustained and the miracles that occurred.

I was going through security in an airport in Jacksonville, Florida, when I was chosen for a random security check. I was still wearing my pressure garments and my headband. My legs were still pretty purple. I was wearing shorts, so you could see the burns on my legs. My uniform was in my luggage, and while I was being checked, a female security officer searched my bags. The male security officer asked me to stretch out my arms, which I did as best I could. As he passed his wand over me, he said, "Sir, may I ask what type of accident you were in?"

"No, it wasn't an accident. It was quite deliberate." His eyes grew huge, and he said, "What do you mean *deliberate?*" I told him, "What was done to me was done to me on purpose."

"What do you mean?"

"I was in the Pentagon on the morning of September 11."

The lady who was screening my luggage now found my uniform jacket. They both stopped what they were doing. They had experienced

9/11, too, although it was on television. They had seen what occurred in the Pentagon, New York City, and Pennsylvania.

The officer lowered his security wand. "We don't need to screen this man," he said. "He's definitely not a terrorist."

I told them, "The Lord has carried us through a very tough challenge in our lives. I've had the opportunity to live. The reason I was here in Jacksonville was to share that story about God's grace in our lives. We still struggle with forgiveness, and we still become angry when we think about the people and organizations that carried out those horrors. But first and foremost we concentrate on God's goodness to us."

In those five-minute conversations I can put a grain of interest in someone's mind to find out more about what I'm saying. Mel can do the same. Because of the gravity of what happened that day, no one looks at us as though we're kooks or idiots—because they experienced 9/11, too. They see my scars. That's authenticity. Everyone can see the authenticity of God's work in our lives and part of that is through the scars we carry—physical, emotional, or spiritual.

We've had so many opportunities to talk to other people about Christ. We talk to anyone who will listen: other burn survivors, our physicians, the media, anybody. Sometimes it doesn't feel very productive. But it plants that seed. Ultimately, we have to plant the seed and let the Holy Spirit convict. We can't take it personally if someone rejects our message. We're doing the job God has called us to do.

★ *Mel*

Even in the hospital when he was in tremendous pain, I watched in amazement as God used Brian to touch a lot of people. When we visited Georgetown Hospital more than a year after he'd been in the emergency room, we met Chaplain Cirillo, the chaplain who prayed with Brian in the emergency room. She knew Brian immediately. With tears in her eyes and much excitement, she told him, "You changed my life. When I was in your presence I felt the presence of the Lord. So seeing you right now, having the chance to meet you, is incredible." Then she turned to me and said, "You just don't know how much God used him to touch my life."

Meeting her and listening to her talk about how God had used Brian brought tears to my eyes. I felt exactly the same way.

★ *Brian*

While I was in the hospital several burn survivors, including Clay Tipton and Walt Roberts, came to visit me. While I didn't know these people, their presence was so comforting and encouraging. They had been through the fire, too. They knew what I was experiencing. They'd felt the pain I felt. I could bond with them in a way I couldn't with anyone else, including Mel.

Another Pentagon survivor, John Yates, and I spent a lot of time together. We didn't know each other before 9/11, but through this crisis we became good friends. Ellen, John's wife, also became a strong support for Mel.

John wasn't as badly burned as I was, so he was released from ICU a week or so earlier. But every morning that I was in step-down care John stopped by to see me.

We joked with each other about how we looked. I knew he looked bad, and he knew I looked worse! The important aspect of my relationship with John was that I had someone with whom I could share my experience. We asked each other the same questions: How did that feel to you? Where were you inside the building? What did you hear? What did you feel? How did you escape? How are you doing in physical therapy?

Although I had Mel, which was great, I had someone else I could talk to about what we were experiencing over the last month in the hospital and what we'd experienced each day. Because John was in better shape than I was, he was always going through things before I did. He was able to encourage me and give me the heads-up on what to expect. In a sense we were members of a special club—a club of burn survivors. And this experience was our rite of initiation.

As time passed, burn survivors would visit me, which was a huge moral boost to me. There was a firefighter who had been burned as severely as I was two years before that, and now he's a body builder. It was amazing to see the recovery he'd made. His visit was so incredibly encouraging.

When he left, I told Mel about the visit and then mentioned to her that I would like to do that someday, to go to other burn survivors and encourage them. We discussed how important it is to do that for the families, too, because they really have no idea what is facing them. That day an idea was planted, and with each burn survivor who visited, the idea took deeper root.

In late February 2002, when I was doing outpatient physical therapy, Amy Brodski, one of my physical therapists, said to me, "Brian, I'd like you to go up and visit one of our patients in intensive care." I told her I would. I was happy to visit him. And I felt Amy's request was a compliment because she knew what I had gone through. She also knew I was a Christian.

The man I visited had been burned in a farm accident. He had a large amount of third-degree burns, mostly around his shoulders. Shoulders are a three-dimensional joint, where you're going up, down, left, right, and then twisting. So I knew he was headed for agonizing pain in physical therapy.

He was wiped out. It was hard to speak with him because he was heavily sedated. I knew the mental anguish he was going through being so heavily medicated. I told him, "You've got the professional character and the heart for hard work. The mission you've got ahead of you is extremely difficult. The staff is asking you to do painful things, such as wearing certain types of garments or enduring certain types of physical therapy. But it's a mission you must accomplish. The staff is not doing things to you or telling you to do things for the sake of curiosity. These people are doing them because they've seen and experienced enough with burns to know how to help you live a good quality of life."

After that I spent the rest of my time talking with his parents. I was able to discuss with them what was ahead, what they should expect, and how they could help their son. Talking with them felt good. I started to think about how this would be a wonderful way to share Christ. I mentioned to Mel that it would be wonderful if we could talk with burn survivors more often.

Most people don't think about burn survivors. We think about cancer or other diseases that may be incurable. The body will heal from a burn, so we don't think about it as being as bad as or worse than surviving cancer. But being burned is a ghastly experience to endure. And only those who have gone through the fire can truly understand the impact of the experience.

In July 2002 a young man placed a pipe bomb in his father's car in Washington, DC. But the brother became the casualty. He went to his dad's car in a parking garage and turned on the ignition. The car blew up, burning the young man on his buttocks and both of his legs. Mel and I were watching the news that night and saw the report. They showed a picture of the man lying on the ground. The fire was out, but they were showing his charred legs to the whole world. Then they did a newscast from the Washington Hospital Center. When the reporter announced, "He's in surgery now," Mel and I looked at each other. We had the exact visual image of what this man was experiencing.

Dale, the nurse practitioner in step-down care, called me three weeks later and asked if I would come to the hospital to visit that young man. He was out of intensive care and in step-down care.

I quickly agreed and decided to go to the Pentagon souvenir shop beforehand to buy a coin with the Army logo on the front. I wanted to have something in hand to give him.

It takes a special will to pull through burns. It's the most excruciating mentally *and* physically challenging injury. It exacts an enormous toll on the survivor, his or her self-perception, and on the family—not to mention the disfigurement factor and the way the rest of the world views the survivor.

We talked a little bit about the types of things he was experiencing, what he was going through, the hallucinations, the different pain levels. I also spoke with his family for more than an hour answering questions about what to expect, what to do, what's normal.

Before I left I handed him a coin as a memento of the visit and told him, "I know you're not in the military, but you've got a tough assignment in front of you right now just like any other soldier gets. That assignment may stink, but you have to get it done. So like a good soldier, get done in here what you have to get done. Listen to what the doctors tell you to do and do it."

In so many words I told him something that Mel told me a lot: You're a soldier. Here's your mission. Get on about it and don't snivel. You don't want to spend the rest of your life being a victim. You have to get past the victim and into the survivor mode.

It was that visit that became the impetus for a serious conversation about starting a ministry.

I went home and told Mel about my experience with that family. "We ought to think about doing this as something more than just a chance opportunity," I told her. "What if we started a ministry specifically to burn survivors and their families? They need someone sympathetic to walk through the experience with them, to tell them what to expect, to encourage them, and to let them know they can make it. Then we can share our story. We can tell them, 'This is what God can do for you because this is what he did for us.'"

We became excited about the possibilities. Our first step was to get a coin design that would represent the ministry so we could give one to each survivor. The coin would represent the coins I received from the Army generals who visited me in the hospital.

Everything seemed to take off from there. Wherever we spoke, we tried to locate a burn unit to visit. Our first visits were to burn units in Lubbock, Texas; Rochester, New York; and Chapel Hill, North Carolina.

★ *Mel*

The ministry has been a blessing, and we've been thrilled to see what God has done through it since its official start in January 2003. We have a real team aspect in our ministry. In organizing and visiting hospitals, Brian has the patient perspective, and I relate to the family members. Even though I watched what he was going through, I didn't physically feel it.

While the ministry has been wonderful, if we had our choice, we would choose the life we had before 9/11. I would never want to face the fire. I think God gave me a gift of ignorance early on so I would be unable to truly understand how critically injured Brian was and how absolutely close to death he was. Had I known those details I don't think I could have kept functioning and been his advocate the way I was.

God knows what he's doing when he hides the future from us. It's a blessing that he doesn't reveal to us any future horrors we may face, because I don't think anybody could handle it. I know I couldn't have said, "Oh yeah, boy, next week my husband's going to get hit by a 757. But hey, that's okay because we're going to start this great ministry!" No way.

★ *Brian and Mel*

Our idea was to visit burn centers and present a care basket to the survivors and their families, filled with items that would have been helpful for us to have while we were in the hospital: devotional books, a Bible, antibacterial wipes to minimize the bacteria (you're constantly washing your hands in a burn unit), and a handmade quilt from Mel as a reminder of our comfort and concern.

We also wanted to be able to offer financial assistance to burn survivors and their families because burns are financially devastating too. Many of these people will never be able to return to work. The more we discussed the possibilities, the more excited we became.

We would name the ministry Face the Fire Ministries, Inc.

Face the Fire Ministries, Inc. has blossomed into speaking opportunities, writing this book, and being able to share our story on a much broader scale than we ever thought we would. That's obviously God's doing; the ministry's success has nothing to do with us. He's just opening doors.

Now that we have started this ministry together and have had the opportunity to visit other burn survivors, we are convinced we've gone through this experience so we can share God's sovereignty, faithfulness, graciousness, and mercy with others who are going through a horrific experience.

We were scheduled to speak at a church in North Carolina on Easter Sunday 2003. The day before the church service, we went down to the Jaycee Burn Unit at the University of North Carolina, Chapel Hill, and made arrangements with the staff to visit some of the patients. The charge nurse told us, "We have a gentleman here who, I think, would benefit from your encouragement." We expected to be there thirty minutes, maybe an hour. We spent almost two hours with the man, mainly listening to him. He had lost his right leg from an electrical burn, had been hospitalized for two months, and was still healing from the burns. He was concerned about so many things, including what he was going to do for a living, and that brought back a lot of memories for us. Then we had the opportunity to talk about our faith in God. We must have piqued his interest because he asked a hospital clergy to visit him after we left.

We believe God really calls us to take the painful experiences of our lives and trust him with them. Then he asks us to take those experiences and help others who are going through the same thing, who need encouragement, and who need to hear about the God of grace.

When we walk into a hospital room, one of the things we try not to acknowledge at first is our burn story. We don't walk in and say, "You know, we're glad to be here. Aren't you privileged to see me? I survived being in the Pentagon." We go in, talk to them, let that meeting be about them, listen to their concerns. And then in the process of hearing so much of the commonality, we're able to describe how we went through the same thing: the pain, nightmares, hallucinations, physical therapy, pain medication, loss of independence, and on and on. Without question, in the course of that conversation they're able to determine our experience stemmed from 9/11. That's when the validity hits them. Here is a couple who have been through this horrible experience together. But we don't start off telling them we're 9/11 survivors.

By the same token, that 9/11 identification is a fast foot in the door with burn units. There's the distinction of surviving the attack on the Pentagon. People welcome us with open arms because they want to know what happened that day in the Pentagon. They want to be part of 9/11. So while we'll tell the staff, we don't talk about that with the burn survivors.

It's been a blessing for us to go to the burn centers. While going out and speaking has been wonderful, the true reward for us is when we go to a burn center and sit and hug family members and talk to the kids or the adults. We share the miracle that God performed in our lives and give them the example of how life can go on and be a quality experience. That's the best part of all—those are the times when we feel that everything we've gone through has been worth it.

TWENTY

Where Was God?

JOURNAL 10/27/01

The medical folks from the Pentagon who triaged him visited. It was awesome. Each person told his or her role in caring for him. Brian told every one of them that he appreciated everything they did for him and they were his angels. Because of their actions, he is a walking miracle. . . . Everyone in the room was crying. . . . What amazing people you assembled, Lord, for such a time as this. Thank you for so totally being in control!

★ *Brian*

Soon after I returned to work, there was a briefing about 9/11 and the damage it had done to the building. One gentleman who was doing a lot of the renovation work said the building would have fared better had the plane entered straight down Corridor 4 because the corridor had more pylons that supported it. I stood up after him and said, "Let me tell you. I'm glad it didn't come in straight down the corridor because I wouldn't be standing here today."

★ *Brian and Mel*

On September 11, 2001, more than three thousand people were brutally murdered. Thousands more were injured. Lives were unalterably changed. Families were ripped apart. And the entire world watched it happen.

When people see that kind of evil so blatantly expressed, many, even Christians, tend to ask, "Where was God?"

As survivors of that day, we can answer that question. We saw God that day—and every day after that.

★ *Brian*

Where was God? He was working to make sure the least amount of people were killed at the Pentagon. On any given day the Pentagon has thirty-thousand or more people working or visiting there, with an estimated twenty-six hundred people in or near the area of impact. The plane was aimed at the only part of the Pentagon that had been fully renovated as part of an eleven-year project to refurbish the sixty-two-year-old building and protect it against attack. There was one wedge of the building that had been newly renovated so there were few people in that area: the E-Ring between Corridors 4 and 5—my ring. There were entire departments that had not moved in yet, so it was the least-occupied wedge of the building.

★ *Mel*

I remember the day I helped Brian unpack his boxes in his new office. He was busy working, and I was bored because he was sifting through documents I couldn't help with. So I sat at his desk and made fun of the Kevlar coating on the windows because it was this yellow-green, weird-looking covering. I don't make fun of that coating anymore! It obviously saved many lives. It kept the glass from shattering and from becoming projectiles.

★ *Brian*

God prompted Pentagon officials several months previous to 9/11 to have a mass casualty exercise to prepare for the event of a major emergency. The scenario they created: a plane hitting the building.

The plane scenario they envisioned was a smaller plane taking off from Reagan National Airport, which is just down the Potomac River from the Pentagon, and experiencing mechanical failure, then crashing in the inner courtyard. Because of that casualty exercise, emergency medical equipment was quickly available and trained medical staff were ready to go to work. So when I arrived at the Redskins snack bar for triage care, I had immediate medical attention, including an IV and morphine shot. That urgent attention saved my life.

★ *Mel*

On September 11, when the World Trade Center was hit, I did something odd, something I would normally never do—I turned off the television. I'm a news junkie, so turning off the television makes no sense to me. I also never called Brian to tell him the news—something else I *always* did. Had I contacted Brian, those moments talking to me would have put him directly in the path of the plane. That was God speaking to me, telling me not to call—to get back to schoolwork with Matt. I'm thankful I actually listened!

God even prepared us for this event months before. Matt had always attended public school. But in March 2001, because of some school situations we decided to homeschool him for a while. Thank God we did. We could not have managed to keep Matt in public school during the months Brian was in the hospital. This was yet another "God thing."

★ *Brian*

I had to use the restroom precisely at the moment that would save my life. If I had remained at my desk, I would have died. There were so many other miracles that show God's hand at work: I survived the blast, being only fifteen to twenty yards from the point of impact. An eighty-ton plane with ten thousand gallons of jet fuel smashed into the building that close to me, causing a fire that had a temperature close to two thousand degrees, and I survived—and was conscious through the entire thing!

I had to be conscious in order to escape because no one was able to rescue me in that corridor. If I'd been unconscious, not only would I have died, but within thirty minutes that part of the building would have collapsed on me. My remains might never have been found.

In the midst of the explosion there was building material flying everywhere—splintered two-by-fours, aluminum framing, sheet rock, concrete, and glass. Yet I received no puncture wounds, and I still have my eyesight and my hearing (although that's diminished).

Many of the sprinklers were damaged because of the crash and lost water pressure because the pipes were not encased to maintain pressure. Many of the water pipes that carry the sprinkler system water in that wedge were damaged. Most of the building damage was done by flooding. Even though many of the sprinkler heads could function, there wasn't enough water pressure behind them to give a good spray. When the E-Ring collapsed, there were even more water pressure breaks at all five floors. Yet I fell under one that was still working. Somehow it wasn't damaged in the blast. The water pressure was sufficient to soak me and extinguish the flames.

Many people tell me I'm lucky to be alive. Mel and I don't consider it luck that I collapsed under a functioning sprinkler system. I think that's where the Lord wanted me to be. You don't survive a 757 flying through the windows and the resulting blast, the fuel, the smoke, the concussion, and the fire.

And most important, I was conscious throughout this whole ordeal. People have told me they thought I must have an incredible pain threshold. And I have replied, "No, I don't think that's it. I think the Lord has an incredible grace threshold," because had I been unconscious, I could say, "Yeah, I got run over by a 757 and woke up three months later in a hospital."

But then there would be no miraculous story to tell. There would be no Christian witness to tell. There would be no family experience to tell. There would be Mel's experience that she could tell because she was conscious through everything.

When I stand up in front of a group of people, show a photograph of the damaged Pentagon, point to where I was in relation to the point of impact, and say I remember it—*that's* an experience to tell.

Many people find it amazing that I walked out of that danger zone. But that was because God was protecting me. While I was saved from burning to death, it was not by virtue of anyone rescuing me. There was only the Lord and me in that corridor.

God placed Roy Wallace and Bill McKinnon in that area to find me. They were the first of many people who offered immense amounts of comfort. God puts people we know, who are familiar to us, to be in the right place at the right time to give us comfort and courage.

There was also Natalie, who stopped to pray with me at the triage site and again outside in the parking lot while I was waiting for an ambulance.

And how is it possible that in a large parking lot, with thousands of people rushing out of the building, trying to get to safety, John Collison just "happened" to help this unknown burn victim—who turned out to be a friend? I needed John to be there with me and to go to the hospital with me. I needed a friendly face—someone I could trust to pass on my ring to Mel and to honor my memory if I were to die. God knew exactly the man and the moment to choose. That was the hand of God putting John right there.

Mel and I don't believe in karma or luck. We don't believe when somebody tells us, "It's nice that those people happened to be where you needed them. What a coincidence." No. Everybody served a purpose throughout my entire evacuation.

★ *Mel*

When the plane hit the building, the Pentagon engineering and maintenance department shut down the power to the damaged part of the building, so that people who were escaping or rescuers wouldn't have to encounter live power lines.

When Bill, Roy, and the other people who rescued Brian from that corridor picked up Brian, they had to go back through the closed access security door. They had to swipe their badge. What made that badge activate a powerless door? There was no electricity to that part of the building. There's really no answer other than the miraculous hand of God opening that door so they were able to evacuate.

Even little things were miracles. Several weeks prior to 9/11 Brian told me he needed new shoes for work and announced he was going to buy leather shoes that cost sixty-five dollars. I'm a cheap person, so I thought, *sixty-five dollars for Army shoes? Are you nuts?* He had never bought leather shoes before, and I couldn't figure out why he wanted them now. But he was adamant about needing *leather* shoes. Those sixty-five-dollar leather shoes saved his feet from burns. Those shoes allowed him to receive the IV in his feet and also allowed me to have a place to touch and rub when he was in pain.

★ *Brian*

Then there was my experience at Georgetown. I was the only casualty taken to that hospital, which was just four miles from the Pentagon. Because the hospital went on Code Orange for disaster alert, they had cleared out all non-life-threatening patients and had already called in all extra available help. I had that entire hospital's undivided attention.

God placed Sergeant Jill Hyson in that Expedition with me. Jill was a reservist, but her civilian job was as an X-ray technician at Georgetown Hospital. She didn't know where Arlington Memorial Hospital was, which was where most of the victims were taken. No one else in that vehicle knew either. The only hospital Jill was confident about finding was Georgetown University Hospital. So that's where we went.

Dr. Williams, the trauma director, was there to work on me in the emergency room. Prior to assuming that position he spent two years at the Washington Hospital Center Burn Unit under Dr. Jordan and Dr. Jeng in a medical residency for trauma. So from the perspective of all the great hospitals in the DC area, not counting the Washington Hospital Center, I was in the emergency room that had the best-trained burn physician in the region, receiving his undivided attention.

When I was moved from the emergency room to their ICU, there were several people on shift that day who specialized in burns: a resident, Sue Jean Kim, who had just completed burn-trauma training at Washington Hospital Center, and Debi Trichel, a burn-specialist nurse with more than ten years of burn-trauma experience. Debi had transferred earlier that year from the Burn Unit at Washington Hospital Center to receive training in cardiac care. Another nurse, Charlotte Almeyer, contacted her sister, a burn unit nurse, to also come help out. According to staff nurse working there, Jeannie Brown, Georgetown ICU had never had a burn patient, since the survivors would naturally be sent to the Burn Unit at Washington Hospital Center.

Again I received undivided attention from people who specialized in giving me exactly what I needed. None of the other nurses in the ICU had burn training.

★*Mel*

Before I discovered the Red Cross was going to pay for the hotel room during Brian's hospital stay, I remember trying to figure out how we were going to afford everything. But again, God stepped in before 9/11, working behind the scenes, preparing me even financially for what I didn't know was ahead.

We've invested through an investment and financial planning group. Brian always wanted me to learn about the financial end of things, but I wasn't interested. I didn't want to attend seminars or talk with financial advisors—mostly because I always felt they talked so condescendingly.

In August, while we were out walking, Brian told me, "I found an agent I think you'll really like. Why don't you go with me to meet her?" I told him okay, then promptly ignored the request. But God kept putting into my mind the thought, *You need to go meet her. Go. Go.*

So after I couldn't ignore the nagging thoughts anymore, I told Brian, "You know, I think I'd like to meet your First Command agent. Why don't you set that up?" Brian was stunned. I said, "I need to know about our finances and insurance if something were ever to happen to you."

A week before the attack, I met Karen Foley. She was a wonderful agent, someone who made me feel comfortable. She gave me her card, which I stuck in my purse . . . and took out the night of September 11, when I called her regarding the medical retirement issue. She handled all our finances so I could concentrate on Brian's condition. I'm not sure what I would have done about our finances had I not listened to God's promptings. He was working even then to prepare us.

Looking back I can see how God was working behind the scenes for months to prepare us for what would happen. For instance, Brian went to work for General Van Antwerp, a strong Christian, who would offer immense comfort and who also became instrumental in making things happen that couldn't have happened without a two-star general, such as the medical retirement issue.

But also there was President Bush. A friend of mine, Bobby Little, and I were talking one day about what a great man George W. Bush is, a man who truly loves God and seeks to honor him. The Bible talks about how leaders are ordained by the Lord. I'm convinced that the Lord gave us President Bush for such a time as this.

President Bush is a man of his word. He stood at Brian's hospital bed and said, "We will get the men who did this. This will not go unanswered." And he has been true to his word.

We pray every day that God will be with him in every decision. That God will lead him and this country to make wise decisions—eternal decisions—even when we look at events and believe they are not good. We don't always understand how God works, but we pray that God would work in President Bush's decisions. It is an honor to pray for him, that he would continue to seek the Lord's wisdom and guidance as he leads our country every day.

While we were in the hospital I did a lot of journaling in the middle of the night and read my Bible constantly. When I was going through a period of questioning God, I read Isaiah 40:28-31:

Do you not know? Have you not heard? The Everlasting God, the Lord, the Creator of the ends of the earth does not become weary or tired. His understanding is inscrutable. He gives strength to the weary, and to him who lacks might He increases power. Though youths grow weary and tired, and vigorous young men stumble badly, yet those who wait for the Lord will gain new strength; they will mount up with wings like eagles, they will run and not get tired, they will walk and not become weary.

Reading those words, I felt was as if God was saying to me, *Daughter, rest. I created the world; you didn't. I'm here. I'm still in control.*

★ *Brian*

There's a passage in the Bible that says, "When you walk through the fire, you will not be scorched, nor will the flame burn you" (Isaiah 43:2). While the damage to my body was physical, the long-term damage was not eternal. In tough situations there may be short-term losses, but we can still keep our eyes on the long-term plan.

There are those who in going through turmoil and chaos demand to know *Why me, God?* They get caught up in the question, *How did you let this happen, God? Where were you?*

But that's the humanistic view of life, the view that says, *I'm the center of attention. I'm the focus. So where were you, God, when I needed you?* The reality is, he is there—even in the worst of circumstances. We're either not looking or not looking hard enough. Or perhaps it's because we expect to see him work according to *our* expectations, not according to his ways and timing.

★*Mel*

As Brian began to tell me the story of his escape from the blast, he only told it piecemeal. The first thing he told me was that he remembered crawling through the hallway terrified that he was going to lose Matthew and me. That was devastating to hear. I would leave after those talks and cry.

As Brian continued to tell me bits and pieces of his story, God began to show me his sovereignty—that he *did* have total control of Brian in the situation and that nothing was going to touch Brian that had not been sifted through God's hands.

There were many times when I would tell God, "I do not like this path, and you need to change it." And God's love for us is so amazing that he would reply, *I understand your anger. I feel it too about what happened to Brian. But I won't change this path. However, I will walk down it with you.*

That wasn't the answer I wanted to hear! But I did find comfort knowing that no matter what I did and said or how belligerent I became with God, he always loved me.

My only recourse was to pray. And the more I prayed, the more I saw answers to my prayers—over all our needs. When Brian's heart rate became dangerously fast, I called everyone I knew to pray. And I would see his heart rate slow. Everything we prayed for God answered almost instantly. It was miraculous to sit and watch that happen. Because God was there.

People say, "Where was God on September 11?" He was in Corridor 4 picking up Brian, knocking him under the sprinkler so the fire would go out, and then picking him up and hauling him down that hallway to get to the people God had picked to be in that spot at that moment to save him. God *was* there. He didn't cause 9/11 to happen. It wasn't God's will. Terrorists, evil men, made a choice with their own free will to murder and destroy. But it's as if God said, *I have given you free will to do evil. I'm angry and saddened that you choose this course, but I will not stop you from your choice. However, I will still have control. I will make my presence known in the miracles that will take place that day.*

And miracles did take place—not only in our story but in many others that took place on 9/11. God placed every person exactly where they needed to be for Brian to escape the Pentagon, to get immediate care, and to live. God was most definitely there—in the Pentagon, in Georgetown, in Washington Hospital Center in the ICU and step-down, and in every part of Brian's healing process.

And he's also most definitely here in the room with you and me. After our experience of walking through the fire and coming out the other side, refined by that very fire, there can be no doubt.

TWENTY-ONE

Looking Ahead

JOURNAL 11/27/01

Father God, your mercies are truly new every morning. Thank you for Brian—not just for giving him to me once, but for renewing our bond by sparing him. It's as though I've received a new gift. He's the truest blessing you've ever given me. What a difference he's made in my life. . . . And for Matt, what a joyous young kid he is. I love him more than I ever knew I could love anyone.

★*Brian*

Our country has, in many ways, begun to move on. The funerals and memorial services are over. War has been declared. Troops have gone to Afghanistan and Iraq. But mostly people have moved on. The intense post-trauma syndrome so many people experienced has waned—as well as interest in what happened that day. Many people can go days without even thinking about 9/11. They forget and think the survivors are doing okay.

But not me. Not my family. Every day I live with the reality of September 11. I've had more than thirty surgeries—five surgeries on my face alone. I may still have to have surgeries to stretch my skin and fix my elbows to get them to extend. I still have occasional pain. For the rest of my life, I will carry scars. There will be a lifetime of adjustments we have to make. There will be things I won't be able to do.

I'm still unable to fully extend my arms. My skin is so tender that it scabs and bleeds and tears. When I first received my skin, the least little bump would make it bleed. My fingers, especially, were so delicate that they would bleed and then swell. While my skin is no longer that sensitive, it still bleeds. I have to be careful when I scratch because my skin is like baby skin—not like calloused forty-year-old skin. My skin blisters doing yard work. It will take time for it to toughen up and become strong.

And there are still days I look in a mirror and wonder where the old Brian has gone—and who is this ghost of a person left in his place.

There are moments when I anxiously turn my eyes upward when a plane passes overhead at the Pentagon. I continue to scan a room for exits. I have restricted outdoor activities to avoid the sun. Since my skin is so sensitive, the last thing I want to do is get sunburned! I no longer have the ability to sense temperature extremes of hot or cold, which is a concern when I run outside during the winter; I could easily get frostbite and not know it.

I rarely cook on the grill; Matt does that now. I start the fireplace, but I just flip a switch because it's gas. While I don't have a huge fear of fire, I'm more guarded about it.

I still struggle physically. A few weeks ago I tried to do a pull-up; I could barely hang from the bar. I couldn't grab it completely, and I didn't have the strength to hold my body weight. I don't know when I'll get that back. I have muscle-tissue loss, both from the fire and from the atrophy of not using my muscles, which means strength loss. I try to lift weights once a week to build bulk back in my arms, stretching them naturally. I can lift about 40 pounds. I can do a modified push-up, but I list to the right a bit.

When I take a two-mile run or do sit-ups, my arms will throb because my blood flow is constricted. My arms have a thinner diameter since I lost so much skin, tissue, and muscle. So there's less room for blood flow, which affects my blood pressure.

Yet there are no daily activities that I can't do right now. I can use the restroom on my own and feed myself. I'm mobile. I can move throughout the house and go up and down stairs. I can drive, which took many painful hours of physical therapy. I can shave myself with a blade—it took almost nine months before I could shave with a blade rather than an electric razor. I can do my own laundry. I'm even able to button the top button of my uniform by myself. And I went from using heavy narcotics to Motrin. That's definitely an improvement!

In January 2003 Dr. Jordan put an incremental cast on my right arm to see if he could get it to straighten out. There was some minor success but not much. We may have to do another surgery some time in the future.

I'm still scarring and getting keloids, thick scars from an excessive growth of fibrous tissue. They look like giant slash scars.

★ Mel

At the six-month anniversary at the White House on March 11, 2002, the survivors and family members of the deceased were sitting together on the South Lawn. Every time a plane would fly overhead, everybody looked up. It was a painful reminder.

I still have moments when fear grips me. In April 2002 we drove through Georgetown to a DC-area Kansas State University alumni association dinner. It was the first time we'd been back to Georgetown. Just driving through those residential streets again brought on a major anxiety attack. I was hyperventilating, trying to drive, and trying to appear calm when I felt as if I was suffocating. It was so intensely uncomfortable to return to Georgetown and relive all those painful memories.

★ Brian

Some days it's difficult to look at myself in a mirror. I look different. Fortunately I don't think it makes any difference to Mel. I know she isn't worried about how I look, which is a good thing! I think I look pretty good for a guy who's been through what we've been through. I had great surgeons who put me back together, and Mel pushed me pretty hard, too. I like to say it was God's strength and Mel's courage driving me through it. She was like a drill instructor about my physical therapy. She'd say, "You're going to get this done. It's just a matter of *when* you decide you're going to get it done. I'm only telling you you're going to get it done." I'm glad Mel cared enough about me to push me to be the best I could be.

As much as I'd prefer to look the way I did before 9/11, in the big picture of things it's not important. I won't have this body for eternity—only for probably another thirty or so years. And this body gives an authenticity to our story when Mel and I walk into a room. When we show up and I look the way I do—with portions of my ears gone, with scars on my face, neck, hands, and arms—people see immediate visible signs of the challenge we've been through. These scars are proof of God's grace in our life—that he did carry us through the fire. But someday I'll have a new body.

★ Mel

My birthday is December 9. On December 10, 2002, Brian was able to take off his pressure garments permanently. I helped him remove those garments, then I gave him my birthday present—his wedding ring to wear again. I wore his ring to help me feel close to him. It was a part of Brian that I could carry with me all the time. It was a wonderful present to be able to say, "This ring is yours again. *You* get to wear it."

★ Brian

I'm no longer comfortable flying. Even the tiniest bit of turbulence has me grabbing the seat in front of me. We flew for the first time after September 11 in April 2002. Mel and I were traveling to Reno, Nevada, to be part of the National Rifle Association's annual convention. We'd been invited to the "honoring heroes" opening ceremony, and then Mel and I were going to speak at the sportsmen's prayer breakfast. While I looked forward to being at the convention, I was nervous about flying to it. Mel had to give me some of my leftover sleep medication to help me sleep the entire flight.

I'm not afraid of flying; I'm just uncomfortable with it. I think the reason is because if the plane should crash, I've already lived through that death. I've lived through the concussion. There are three ways to die in a plane crash. If you're fortunate, the traumatic impact will kill you first. If you live through that, then you have to live through the fire. If you live through that, you have to live through the smoke. I've experienced all three. As bad as that experience was, flying with Mel and Matt is worse because if something did happen to our plane, I already know the horror of that type of death. And I don't want them to experience that—nor do *I* particularly want to experience it again.

People often ask me if I've forgiven Osama bin Laden, the terrorists, and the other accomplices involved in 9/11. Honestly, I have to say no. I don't say that with great pride but out of truthfulness. It's my responsibility as a Christian to work toward forgiveness. But I'm not there yet. It's a daily process. Yet, I'm not bitter.

When I look where I've been and where I am now, God is absolutely gracious. So if I were bitter now, after having come through the last three years, that bitterness would be grossly displaced.

Do I desire to see justice served? Absolutely! But do I sit and stew or bemoan my altered life? No. We serve a magnificent God. As a Christian I work through the process of forgiving those who hurt me because I know ultimately God will judge rightly and the people who chose evil will receive their just reward. Knowing that God will handle the judgment, I don't have to harbor feelings for revenge. Mel and I accentuate our relationship with God, not our hatred or our unforgiveness of the organizations that have supported this type of evil.

And yet it's going to take a long time to forgive and move on. This is probably the toughest part of my faith. I'm learning how to forgive when forgiveness doesn't come easily. I think it will take years for me to completely forgive Osama bin Laden and his minions. As long as I maintain Christ as my center, I'm confident there will be a day when I can forgive the terrorists and Osama bin Laden. I still deal with anger toward them—especially when I read something new about them or see photos of bin Laden, Mohammad Atta, or the eighteen other hijackers. But I try not to dwell on it. I continue to live my life to the best of my ability, for that's the best way for me to get to the point of forgiveness.

So even though I continue to have a great zeal for justice, the best example Mel and I can give is not one of hatred toward our enemies. Instead, we recognize that what these people intended for evil the Lord has turned into good. It's been a rough experience to get to this point. But when we tell our story, it's an extremely positive, faith-oriented story. We want people to hear our story and think, *There has to be something to this, for somebody to have gone through these types of challenges and still be able to say the Lord was with them.*

★*Mel*

I don't struggle as much with unforgiveness as Brian does because I just don't focus on it. I choose not to think about it. I know the ultimate justice is God's justice—and he will handle it.

Matt still struggles with anger and unforgiveness. He's asked me a few times, "Could Dad still die?" He is so afraid of that and is very protective of Brian. Brian and I try to let him know how much we love him and that we're all going through this *together*.

For a little more than a year Matt talked constantly about what he'd like to do to Osama bin Laden. He would tell me, "If I was in a room with Osama bin Laden, he would not leave the room." We don't hear him say that much anymore. I think he's grown out of it. He realizes that life is good. What happened to his dad was a horrible thing. It's not a problem we've forgotten. But it's a problem that we, as citizens of this nation, have delegated to the responsibility of the federal, state, and local authorities. And in the meantime while they're working on the war on terror, we're living our lives. I think probably a big part of that, too, is that as a nation we're moving away from 9/11. It's not constantly in Matt's face as it was. He doesn't have to dwell on it day in and day out.

Matt had some difficult times while we were writing this book. One night as we discussed what we wanted to include, Matt walked into the room and overheard us talking about what Brian experienced in the Pentagon. Matt started to cry and ran from the room. It's still a tender subject for him, and probably will be for the rest of his life.

Brian underwent counseling with our pastors to work through the spiritual issues of our experience. I never went to counseling until I realized we were going to write this book. I knew it was going to be very emotionally overwhelming to revisit all of the details. There are times when I can talk about the story and be completely emotionally detached from it, not even feel anything. Then there are times I can think about it and spend the day sobbing. So I thought, *Okay, I'm either going to handle this as a mental meltdown, or I've got to deal with this.* So I dealt with it. I found a Christian counselor who helped me work through a lot of strategies in dealing with my anger. She also helped me to see that I had a lot more trauma in my life than I realized. She was a good sounding board and helped me work through some coping mechanisms to handle the experience of revisiting the horrors in graphic detail all over again. She encouraged me to be honest and to allow myself to feel the things I had not allowed myself to feel, because at the time I didn't have the strength to take care of Matt and Brian and deal with my own issues.

I think we're far more in tune with each other now than we were before because I became accustomed to anticipating his needs. We're much more relaxed than we were before too. I think probably one of the greatest things that has come out of this is Brian's sense of humor, because he really didn't have one before the attack. Matthew called him "Fun Fighter McDoom" or "Mr. Negativity." He was always serious.

There were always the *thou shalt nots* rather than the *thou shalts*. He was always finding the lesson or the theology in something and accentuating the serious side of life. Recently Matt earned some money that he wanted to spend at the mall, but it was late in the evening. Before 9/11 Brian would never have taken him to the mall. Going that late wasn't pragmatic, and the trip may have been too much fun! But this time we went—as a family. And that's just one small example of how Brian has lightened up.

★ *Brian*

I've also tried to relax my old drill-instructor style of fathering Matt. I'm more conscious of how I come across to him. I try to laugh more with him. I'm learning what's critical and what isn't.

I've even learned to laugh at myself. It puts me—and others—at ease.

Several months ago I called my friend Steve Ener. He told me, "Your ears must be burning. I was just thinking about you."

I started to laugh and said, "Oh man, don't say, '*ears are burning*.'"

Mel and I also laughed about my arms when both of them were still not extending fully. They were almost at a ninety-degree angle. So when I would go shopping with Mel, I would tease her and say that she liked me to go shopping with her because she could put her purse over my right arm and the clothes she was going to try on over my left arm, and it took no effort for me to hold them. They were frozen in that position.

I like that I'm not as uptight anymore. I appreciate my family much more because of this horrific experience. Mel and I have been married more than sixteen years, and we have always had a strong relationship. Yet we were also like a lot of couples—snapping from time to time, then apologizing. We still argue over whether to have pizza or burgers, about whether we can afford something. But now we really *cherish* our time together. And I *always* think about how I say good-bye to her in the mornings.

★ Mel

My relationship with God is stronger than it has ever been. Is the intensity the same now as during those most critical days? Sadly, no. I miss the closeness I had with God, but I am still growing and learning every day.

I spoke with a friend of mine whose husband died a few years ago, and she said she went through the same thing spiritually. We both had an intense relationship with God during those crisis moments, when we felt God's presence around us continually. But as Brian healed, I seemed to depend less and less on God, which is wrong and I know it. While I completely depended on God in the lowest of valleys, the mountaintop experiences of life are where I take him for granted at times. I miss the spiritual focus I had with God at the time. But I don't miss dealing—on a minute-by-minute basis—with the tragedy.

★ Brian

I can assure you that if there were any way I could have avoided all this, I would have. I am very proud of my Purple Heart, but I'd trade it for the Brian of September 10 in a second.

So many people have asked us: Because of the ministry we now have, because of the way God is using our story, is it worth it?

Would I still have done this if I knew the plane was coming? And the answer is easily no.

Yet I can also answer yes. If what Mel and I have experienced causes even one person to make a decision to become a Christ follower, then it was worth it.

While it hasn't been a pleasant experience by any means, ultimately I know that in the course of eternity this life is like a poof of wind. If one person begins a relationship with Christ because of my experiences and I'm stuck with this body for the next thirty years, what's thirty years with this body knowing that another person will join me in heaven for eternity? While we would never have chosen this path, the Lord allowed us to have this experience, and we're responding as faithful followers of Jesus.

★ *Mel*

When people ask me, "Was it worth it?" I easily and without hesitation answer, "Absolutely." Even through all that pain, I learned a lesson about God's sovereignty. It has deepened my faith and my relationship with God, and it has given me an opportunity to share Christ boldly. Our church's three tenets are:

1. Seek him constantly.
2. Serve him faithfully.
3. Share him boldly.

This experience has given me the opportunity to put those tenets to work.

It has also been an opportunity for Matt to see what putting feet to your faith means and to see the truth of what God can do in your life. As a twelve-year-old he witnessed some mighty miracles in his parents' lives. And he experienced them too. This ordeal is going to be a testimony of how God's going to use him through all of this.

★ *Brian*

I'm not sure what the future holds. After twenty years in the military, I'm set to retire from the Army in 2004. While I'll miss being a soldier, I realize I can no longer fully complete the duties the Army requires. I've loved being in the Army. It has provided a good career and many opportunities to fulfill my interests and abilities. But with the retirement, Mel and I will be able to focus completely on working with Face the Fire Ministries, Inc. My public speaking is the best contribution I can make both to my faith and to the Army.

I know God has a purpose for my life. God continues to open doors and show me glimpses of what he has for me to do. I'm committed to yield every day to his will.

★*Mel*

I've always been a news junkie, but now I have a *need* to know what's happening in the world. Other than that, my life is back to normal. Once Brian was able to do things for himself again, my life returned to being a wife and a mom instead of a caregiver.

Matt's going to public school now. I enjoy quilting, having lunch with friends, and attending a weekly Bible study. Life is good once again.

Debi Davis, a friend of mine who took me back and forth from the hospital many times, arranged to have my house cleaned, and prayed and visited us consistently, walked up to me after our church's 2002 Memorial Day service. It was the first Memorial Day service after 9/11 and was a very emotionally difficult and draining day for our family. Debi put her arm around me and whispered in my ear, "Sometimes the ultimate sacrifice doesn't involve giving your life. It could be giving a lot of other things, too." She's right. Brian has given almost all he had for his country, short of his life. That is our ultimate sacrifice.

ACKNOWLEDGMENTS

JOURNAL ENTRY 10/5/01
I praise you, God, for all the people you have used, your chosen angels, to spare Brian, to pull him from that inferno.

We are so grateful and indebted to the following people:

Matt Birdwell: Son, thank you for always being a trooper and for understanding. God will use you in mighty ways! We love you.
Americans of faith who prayed for our family
B&B Media, Tina Jacobson, Vicki Andrews, and staff
Shirley Baldwin, for your friendship and love
Col. (Dr.) John Baxter
Col. Robin Davitt
Capt. (Dr.) Brandon Goff
TSgt. Jill Hyson
Cpl. Dan Nimrod
Spc. Kris Sorenson
Lt. Col. (Dr.) Dave Kristo, Walter Reed Army Medical Center
Georgetown University Hospital, Dr. Michael Williams, and staff
Washington Hospital Center, Dr. Marion Jordan, Dr. James Jeng, and the awesome Burn Center staff
Dennis and Joyce Boykin, for years of friendship and caring for our puppy
Maj. John Collison, for being the ring bearer in the emergency room
Col. Robert Cortez
The guys who carried me (Brian) out of Corridor 4 in the Pentagon:
    Lt. Col. Bill McKinnon
    Col. Karl Knoblauch
    Col. John Davies
    Lt. Col. Thomas Cleary
    Lt. Col. Gerald Barrett
    Col. Roy Wallace
Paul and Holly Fine

Charles and Eloise Clarke, for loving me (Mel) even though your pain was so great. You gave me a wonderful blessing by allowing me to spend so much time with you. I love you.

The Fronks: Connie, thanks for being there for us.

Immanuel Bible Church, Pastor Michael Easley, the staff, and body of believers. What an incredible witness you are for Jesus Christ.

Dennis Jernigan and Shepherd's Heart Music for your friendship and gift of music

Kansas City Chiefs NFL Club and their great fans

Gen. John Keane, for your "muddy boots" hugs

Karen Mann: I (Mel) love you, friend. Thanks for all the prayers, tears, and middle-of-the-night phone calls.

Jan Menig, for giving up your tee time to be at the hospital

Natalie Ogletree, for being the most precious gift God gave us in our most desperate time of need

My (Brian's) mom, Loretta, and stepfather Patrick Reves, for training me up as a child should go, according to Proverbs 22:6

Col. Dane Rota, for being a great big brother. Thanks for everything and for always being there when I (Mel) needed you most.

Gen. Eric and Patty Shinseki, for your leadership, friendship, and constant encouragement

The United States Army, for a great twenty years

Dept. of the Army Public Affairs team, for their service

Scott and Debbie Vance: Thanks, friends. We love you. That's all.

Maj. Gen. Robert Van Antwerp, for being a great godly influence and for all our Saturday morning visits

Kathryn Weeden and the Senate Page school

Capt. Calvin Wineland, the NASCAR wannabe

The YOU Sisters, my (Mel's) great friends who supported me through this crazy time. Thanks for your love and encouragement. YOU are the best!

Fellow burn survivors

John, Tick, Louise, Kevin, Juan, Dave, and Wayne

and

THE GREAT PHYSICIAN, JESUS CHRIST

Brian, Mel, and Matt. Copyright © 1999 by Campus Photo.

Aerial view of the Pentagon following the terrorist attack of 9/11. Courtesy of Department of Defense, Pentagon Force Protection Agency.

The Pentagon following the terrorist attack—X marks the spot of impact. Brian's office window is circled. Courtesy of Department of Defense, Pentagon Force Protection Agency.

President George W. Bush thanks Dr. Marion Jordan, Director of the Burn Center at the Washington Hospital Center. Copyright © 2001, *Washington Post* photo by Bill O'Leary. Reprinted with permission.

President Bush as he leaves Brian's ICU room at the Washington Hospital Center. Courtesy of George A. Sample, M.D., FCCP.

Washington Redskins Jeff George and Chris Samuels visit Brian in the ICU. Copyright © 2001 by Leslie E. Kossoff/LK Photos.

First Lady Laura Bush, President Bush, and Brian share a "Texan moment" at the White House prior to the Concert for America. Courtesy of The White House, photograph by Susan Sterner.

President Bush and Brian exchange salutes in the diplomatic reception area at the White House. Courtesy of The White House, photograph by Susan Sterner.

Brian, Mel, and Bob Lepine of FamilyLife Ministries celebrating the presentation of the Robertson McQuilkin Award for Commitment in Marriage to Mel. Copyright © 2002 by FamilyLife. Reprinted with permission.

All other photographs used by permission from the Birdwell family collection. All rights reserved.

RESOURCES

Books
Munster, Andrew M., M.D., and Glorya Hale. *Severe Burns: A Family Guide to Medical and Emotional Recovery.* The Johns Hopkins University Press, 1993.

Yancey, Philip. *Where Is God When It Hurts?* Zondervan, 1990.

Swindoll, Charles R. *Why, God?* Word Publishing Group, 2001.

Web sites
Immanuel Bible Church
www.immanuelbible.net

Includes a link to the video the church took of Brian in the hospital. This video was shown at the church's Thanksgiving 2001 service.

Burn-related resources
Tampa General Hospital Regional Burn Center
http://www.tgh.org/sections/03_services/centers/centers.htm

The Phoenix Society for Burn Survivors, Inc.
http://www.phoenix-society.org
http://www.burnsurvivor.org/

National Center for the Dissemination of Disability Research
(This is a great resource to familiarize yourself with burn rehab.)
http://www.ncddr.org/rr/burn/burnguide.html

American Burn Association
www.ameriburn.org

SCRIPTURES FOR COMFORT

We leaned on these verses for comfort and strength through the dark days of Brian's hospital stay.

"Have I not commanded you? Be strong and courageous! Do not tremble or be dismayed, for the Lord your God is with you wherever you go." Joshua 1:9

He keeps the feet of His godly ones, but the wicked ones are silenced in darkness; for not by might shall a man prevail. Those who contend with the Lord will be shattered; against them He will thunder in the heavens, the Lord will judge the ends of the earth; and He will give strength to His king, and will exalt the horn of His anointed. 1 Samuel 2:9-10

Now I know that the Lord saves His anointed; He will answer him from His holy heaven, with the saving strength of His right hand. Psalm 20:6

The Lord is my light and my salvation; whom shall I fear? The Lord is the defense of my life; whom shall I dread? Psalm 27:1

The Lord is their strength, and He is a saving defense to His anointed. Psalm 28:8

The Lord will give strength to His people; the Lord will bless His people with peace. Psalm 29:11

The Lord looks from heaven; He sees all the sons of men; from His dwelling place He looks out on all the inhabitants of the earth, He who fashions the hearts of them all, He who understands all their works. The king is not saved by a mighty army; a warrior is not delivered by great strength. . . .
Behold, the eye of the Lord is on those who fear Him, on those who hope for His lovingkindness, to deliver their soul from death and to keep them alive in famine. Our soul waits for the Lord; He is our help and our shield. For our heart rejoices in Him, because we trust in His holy name. Let Your lovingkindness, O Lord, be upon us, according as we have hoped in You. Psalm 33:13-16, 18-22

God is our refuge and strength, a very present help in trouble. Psalm 46:1

Ascribe strength to God; His majesty is over Israel and His strength is in the skies. O God, You are awesome from Your sanctuary. The God of Israel Himself gives strength and power to the people. Blessed be God! Psalm 68:34-35

My flesh and my heart may fail, but God is the strength of my heart and my portion forever. Psalm 73:26

He who dwells in the shelter of the Most High will abide in the shadow of the Almighty. I will say to the Lord, "My refuge and my fortress, my God, in whom I trust!" For it is He who delivers you from the snare of the trapper and from the deadly pestilence. He will cover you with His pinions, and under His wings you may seek refuge; His faithfulness is a shield and bulwark.

You will not be afraid of the terror by night, or of the arrow that flies by day; of the pestilence that stalks in darkness, or of the destruction that lays waste at noon. A thousand may fall at your side and ten thousand at your right hand, but it shall not approach you. You will only look on with your eyes and see the recompense of the wicked. For you have made the Lord, my refuge, even the Most High, your dwelling place. No evil will befall you, nor will any plague come near your tent.

For He will give His angels charge concerning you, to guard you in all your ways. They will bear you up in their hands, that you do not strike your foot against a stone. You will tread upon the lion and cobra, the young lion and the serpent you will trample down.

"Because he has loved Me, therefore I will deliver him; I will set him securely on high, because he has known My name. He will call upon Me, and I will answer him; I will be with him in trouble; I will rescue him and honor him. With a long life I will satisfy him and let him see My salvation." Psalm 91

The Lord reigns, He is clothed with majesty; the Lord has clothed and girded Himself with strength; indeed, the world is firmly established, it will not be moved. Psalm 93:1

For the Lord is a great God and a great King above all gods, in whose hand are the depths of the earth, the peaks of the mountains are His also. Psalm 95:3-4

Splendor and majesty are before Him, strength and beauty are in His sanctuary. Psalm 96:6

On the day I called, You answer me; You made me bold with strength in my soul. Psalm 138:3

O God the Lord, the strength of my salvation, You have covered my head in the day of battle. Psalm 140:7

The way of the Lord is a stronghold to the upright, but ruin to the workers of iniquity. Proverbs 10:29

By wisdom a house is built, and by understanding it is established; and by knowledge the rooms are filled with all precious and pleasant riches. A wise man is strong, and a man of knowledge increases power. For by wise guidance you will wage war, and in abundance of counselors there is victory. Proverbs 24:3-6

Trust in the Lord forever, for in God the Lord, we have an everlasting Rock. For He has brought low those who dwell on high, the unassailable city; He lays it low, He lays it low to the ground, He casts it to the dust. The foot will trample it, the feet of the afflicted, the steps of the helpless. The way of the righteous is smooth; O Upright One, make the path of the righteous level. Isaiah 26:4-7

And He will be the stability of your times, a wealth of salvation, wisdom and knowledge; the fear of the Lord is his treasure. Isaiah 33:6

"If anyone is thirsty, let him come to Me and drink. He who believes in Me, as the Scripture said, 'From His innermost being will flow rivers of living water.'" John 7:37-38

And my God will supply all your needs according to His riches in glory in Christ Jesus. Philippians 4:19

*Face the Fire Ministries, Inc. seeks
to assist burn survivors, as well as
our servicemen and women who
are wounded in combat, their
families, and the medical facilities
that specialize in their care.*

Healing from such traumatic
injuries is a long and arduous process. Our hope is to provide comfort for those facing such difficult
physical, emotional, and spiritual
challenges. Through these efforts
we hope that others are healed,
strengthened, and encouraged as
we labor in the Spirit and power of
our true Savior and the Great Physician, Jesus Christ.

To learn how to help minister
to those in need please contact:

Face the Fire Ministries, Inc.
P.O. Box 2798
Woodbridge, VA 22195-2798
(571) 278-5103
www.facethefire.org

LTC (RET) BRIAN BIRDWELL, a Distinguished Military Graduate of Lamar University, has served at Ft Sill OK, the Republic of Korea (South Korea), Ft Riley KS, and the Federal Republic of Germany (from where he was deployed to Operation Desert Shield/Desert Storm). He earned the Bronze Star for action in the Gulf War. Later he served at Ft Leavenworth KS, Ft Lewis WA, and returned to Ft Leavenworth to attend Command and General Staff College. On 9-11 he was serving on the Department of the Army staff at the Pentagon as the Executive Officer to the Deputy Assistant Chief of Staff for Installation Management. Since his recovery, he has appeared on *The Oprah Winfrey Show,* ABC's *Nightline,* CBN, CNN, and FOX News Channel.

MEL BIRDWELL, a graduate of Kansas State University, has had extensive experience in working with programs for senior citizens in Kansas and in Washington. In June 2002 she was presented with the fourth annual Robertson McQuilkin Award for Commitment to Marriage by FamilyLife. Brian and Mel have been married for seventeen years and have a fifteen-year-old son, Matthew.

GINGER KOLBABA, managing editor of *Marriage Partnership* magazine, a publication of Christianity Today International, is the author of *Dazzled to Frazzled and Back Again—the Bride's Survival Guide* (Revell) and more than 100 magazine articles. She and her husband, Scott, live in Illinois.